EDUCATION: Planning and Human Development

EDUCATION

Planning and Human Development

(In 8 Volumes)

Teaching in a Technology-rich Environment

(Volume 6)

V.C. Pandey

ISHA BOOKS

DELHI—110 033

EDUCATION: Planning and Human Development
(Education)

Rs. 7000 (Set in 8 Vols.)

ISBN: 81-8205-006-5 (Set)
ISBN: 81-8205-012-X (Vol. 6)

Published in 2003 in India by
Isha Books, D-43, Prithviraj Road
Adarsh Nagar, Delhi-110 033

Lasertypesetting by: Varsha Graphics, Delhi
Printed at: Chawla Offset Printers, Delhi

Preface

The information age brings wonderful opportunities and new challenges to the system of education. Technology provides educators with the opportunity to move from simply streamlining the way things have always been done to really imagining things they would like to do. In a technology-rich classroom, students don't "learn" technology. Technology merely provides the tools to be used for authentic learning.

Technology in schools needs to serve as a tool to transform teaching and learning. The learners of all ages should be empowered with the skills needed to be successful in an ever-changing world. Teachers must determine how technology tools are used, and they must have a hand in designing the staff development process that trains them. They must work together to create exemplary units, and then they must share their experiences with one another. They must take responsibility for helping design the staff development process so that it really meets their needs — so that it includes time to practice using the equipment, to watch teachers model lessons that infuse technology into the curriculum, and to mentor other teachers.

In order to successfully infuse technology into their classrooms, teachers must have the support of all stakeholders in the educational community. They must resist the notion that learning to use the "gadgets" is an end in itself. They must provide desperately needed leadership to find the best ways of using technology to enhance teaching and learning. They must expect and demand the best and most interesting software to enhance their educational goals.

This book provides practical ways to use technology in the classroom. It will be a highly beneficial reference tool for students, teachers, academicians and policy makers of this technology-driven world.

Editor

Contents

1

Impact of Technology in Education

Technology provides educators with a way to individualize and customize the curriculum to match learners' developmental needs and also provide a nonthreatening and motivating environment for repetitious learning tasks. In classrooms where technology is used, students interact more with their peers and teachers than in traditional classrooms. Students change the manner in which they organize and accomplish their work, choosing to work collaboratively to solve complex problems. Collaboration becomes a learning tool, a means to an end, not just a chance for students to socialize.

Technology provides powerful tools for organizing and analyzing information and modeling concepts and underlying structures. Students who have the opportunity to use these tools gain a deeper understanding of complex topics and concepts and are more likely to be able to recall information later in life and use it to solve prob-lems in nonschool situations. One of the most important contributions technology makes in the classroom is how it affects students' attitudes toward learning.

Technology offers greater opportunities for learner control and greater connections between class work and the real world. Technology encourages students to take charge of their education. In classrooms where technology is part of the curriculum, students are more likely to initiate learning-based activities, sometimes even directing them. In addition to exploring topics more often on their own, students who regularly use laptops assume a greater variety of roles in the learning process, helping to teach other students and even their teachers. In general, students respond positively when given the chance to actively participate in the learning process via technology. By giving students greater control of their education and increasing their motiva-tion to explore and discover, technology plays a major role in instilling in students a love of learning that will help them to reach new heights of achievement not only in school, but throughout their lives.

The keys to raising student achievement are to provide students with a solid foundation of basic skills and to motivate them to learn. Technology can help accomplish this goal. It engages stu-dents and fires their imaginations. It helps teachers stimulate young minds in ways that make a profound and lasting difference. Once students become familiar with technology, they quickly develop proficiency in its use. This opens up an exciting new world of learning possibilities for them, and their potential for achievement skyrockets. Students gain new skills and become familiar with new technologies that will help prepare them for future success in an increasingly technological world. Even the most basic tools can help young learners become more productive.

Technology helps students create work that looks more professional. So when it's time to hand in or publish their work, students take pride in sharing it with their peers, parents, and teachers. In the classroom, many teachers are turning to digital media to strengthen students' basic skills. Using video and audio technology brings class material to life in a way that stimulates young minds and facilitates learning. By incorporating pictures, sound, and animation, multimedia significantly enhances students' ability to recall basic facts, as well as improving their understanding of complex systems. One reason for this improvement may be that digital media tools can be used to address each student's individual learning style, thereby empowering all students to achieve their potential. Gaining technological proficiency helps students learn more effectively, and it also improves their desire to learn.

The introduction of technology will not in itself improve the quality of education, there are several ways in which it can be used as a powerful tool in addressing the problems. One of the earliest insights into the educational applications of technology was that interactive computer-based systems admit the possibility of individualizing the educational process to accommodate the needs, interests, proclivities, current knowledge, and learning styles of each particular student. Even the earliest drill-and-practice based computer-assisted instruction systems, in which th student was exposed to successive blocks of textual material and answered aseries of questions posed by the computer, typically offered the advantages of self-paced instruction. Among other things, self-pacing obviates the need for teachers to target their presentations to some hypothetical "typical" pupil, leaving part of the class behind while other students become bored, restless and inattentive.

Significance of Technological Knowledge

Technological knowledge can be divided into procedural knowledge which relates to the activity, and conceptual knowledge which relates to the body of content. There is probably more international agreement among technology educators about the activity of technology than about the content of technology. This is a helpful separation to make when designing curriculum and discussing teaching, but it is not a separation which should be evident to the students. Students should perceive technology as a thoroughly integrated activity, not one which can be separated into content and process, or theory and practice. Some curriculum documents separate these two areas of knowledge.

While the traditional focus of technology education has been on activity, i.e., on doing and making things, this has represented a narrow interpretation of procedural knowledge. This focus has not been accompanied by an emphasis on all aspects of procedural knowledge, but has typically been concerned with those procedures most closely aligned with the development of manipulative skills and how to use tools effectively and safely. A relatively recent realisation has been that there are many significant cognitive skills which areimportant for students to develop, and which are suitable to be developed in the unique context of technology education. The term unique is appropriate because there is no other curriculum area in which students have as significant an opportunity to think and reflect and develop ideas, and then to test their ideas in a practical context.

Procedural knowledge is developed through the creation of a process, as when a solution to a particular need or brief is sought. There are a range of these processes which are utilised in the development of technology and therefore may also be appropriate in teaching technology, the two most common being design and problem solving.

As with technology, and even more specifically with design in technology, studies of scientists at work seem to indicate that there is no generalisable method. The notion that there is a common series of steps followed by all research scientists, such as defining the problem, gathering information, forming a hypothesis, making observations, testing hypotheses, and drawing conclusions, is not generally held. One of the reasons for the continued perpetration of this myth is the way in which results are presented in research journals. The standardised style of presentation makes it appear that all scientists follow a standard research plan.

There is a range of activities in which students are engaged when they "do" technology. They do not necessarily do all the activities every time they complete a task, and certainly do not do them in the same order every time. The activities depend on the nature of the student and the nature of the problem. There are many activities in this process, but the most important include: evaluation, communication, modelling, generating ideas, research and investigation, producing documenting. It may be appropriate that these activities be called aspects rather than stages of the process; stages has sequential connotation which is not appropriate as a technology process. If these aspects are standardised and sequenced for all students for all projects, then it is not possible to achieve the goal of revealing the cognitive development of students through the documentation of their design process.

This is the case because they are being forced into a way of thinking that has been predetermined by the teacher. Their cognitive development is neither revealed nor encouraged. These activities are not ends in themselves, but rather are done and practised in order to achieve other goals. These other goals include students becoming independent problem solvers, becoming creative and reflective, and becoming critical and expressive; that is, the goals are achievement of the generic competencies that all students need and should have upon leaving school. The situation in Western Australia is representative of more global thinking about the nature of the processes of technology. There has been a move away from the notion of a prescribed process such as Design-Make-Appraise to the idea that there is a range of processes in which students are engaged when they do technology.

Design is justifiably the most common and popular of the processes appropriate to technology education, and has been identified as such in the US Standards for Technology Education. In the real world it is a significant process in the development of technology in many disciplines from engineering to architecture, and from an educational perspective it is an ideal methodology to use as a vehicle to achieve the desired competencies. There is very little research about design, and therefore very little informed guidance on how to teach it. But there is some. There seems to be no simple generalisable process. "The processes involved in designing are not linear, they do not always start from human needs, and they do not always proceed in an orderly way. They are reiterative, spiralling back on themselves, proceeding by incremental change and occasional flashes of insight".

Research has been conducted on both expert designers and children doing design in a technology education context with some parallels in the findings. What students do when they design in technology is a very convoluted and complex process, and is different every time they design something. Studies of designers working in technological fields also reject the notion that what they do can be represented by an algorithm. So both seem to adopt inventive and flexible approaches which are adapted to the situation in which they are working. Individuals also seem to have preferences for how they design. In the design situation where teachers insist on progressing through set stages, students in fact adopt their own strategies in order to get the job done, but ritualistically use the teacher's approach to satisfy assessment demands. For example in the common requirement to sketch four design alternatives to a problem or brief, a student is often interested in only one, and does the others just to satisfy the teacher.

The appeal of problem solving as a methodology lies in the fact that it is a natural activity; humans have always been faced with problems and tried to solve them. In this sense it is also a useful model for understanding technological development in that it can incorporate the broad range of variables involved in the solution to a technological problem. Despite the fact that the terms design and problem solving are often used interchangeably, problem solving is different from design in that design deals with ill defined problems and may not begin with a problem, while of course problem solving does. It is helpful to clarify different types of problem solving. McCormick identified three types of problem solving:

i) a general problem solving approach referring to the process more than the problem itself.

ii) a global problem referring to a significant problem, the solution to which will take some time.

iii) emergent problems which arise throughout any process and must be overcome in order to proceed.

A systems approach is often placed in a problem solving context. For example, in many technology curricula in the USA a system is represented as a solution to a problem. A systems approach may be either analytical, and thereby used as a way of viewing the world or a specific context or object, or functional in that a systems process is followed for diagnostic or production purposes. Many generic groups of systems are represented in the literature. Examples include structural, mechanical, electronic, communication, production, transportation and biotechnological systems. These systems represent much of technology, and are often used to reduce a technology to a simple graphic model that illustrates basic elements.

Information Technology in Classrooms

Researchers and practitioners in the field of educational technology are already convinced that information technologies have the potential not only to imrove the efficacy of current teaching methods, but perhaps more importantly, to support fundamental changes in those methds that could have important implicatons for the next generation. Although technological change in the computer industry is difficult to predict with any certainty, a useful life of between three and five yearsmay represent a realistic expectation for schools, assuming that the criteria for replacement include not only age-related malfunction, but also obsolescence and the inability to support then-current software.

In US about 20 percent of all school computers were connected to a LAN, though nearly a third of all elementary schools and one-half of all high schools reported that at least some of their computers were interconnected in this manner. The use of LANs for instructional purposes would also appear to be enjoying a period of unusually rapid increase. About half of all public schools had at least one connection to the Internet as of fall 1995, and another 11 percent to a wide area network that was not connected to the Internet. Although it is encouraging that 61 percent of schools are now connected to wide area networks (WANs) allowing at least some form of communication with remote sites, these connections are used only modestly by teachers, and are often unavailable for use by students.

Until greater external network bandwidth becomes more widely available within the schools, many Internet applications having an extensive audio and/or graphical component will remain too slow for practical use. Among the principal determinants of the extent to which American schools are able to make use of the Internet and other wide area networks is the availability of reasonably priced telecommunications services of adequate bandwidth to support the interactive use of network-based applications.

Among the earliest applications of computer technology within the field of education were systems designed to automate certain forms of tutorial learning. Such systems, which were first deployed on an experimental basis during the 1960s, are commonly referred to using the (now confusingly general) term computer-assisted instruction (CAI). In a classical CAI application, short blocks of instructional material are presented to an individual student, interspersed with questions designed to test that student's comprehension of specific elements of the material. Questions must typically be posed within a multiple-choice or "true/false" framework, or in such a way as to admit a simple, concrete answer that can be interpreted by the system in a straightforward manner.

Feedback is generally provided to the student as to the accuracy of his or her responses to individual questions, and often as to the degree of mastery demonstrated within a given content area. Such systems generally also support "branched" structures, in which the student's performance on one question, or degree of mastery of one content area, determines the sequence, and in some cases, the level of difficulty, of the instructional material and questions that follow. Additional time can then be spent on material with which the student is having difficulty, while avoiding needless repetition of subject matter that has already been mastered. More "intelligent" CAI systems may be capable of inferring a more detailed picture of what the student does and does not yet understand, and of actively helping to diagnose and "debug" the student's misapprehensions and erroneous conceptual models.

If a student is having difficulty learning to subtract, for example, the computer may recognize that he or she is systematically failing to "borrow a one," making it possible to offer specific coaching rather than a simple repetition of the original instructional material. While promising early examples of such systems have already been demonstrated in such content areas as mathematics and computer programming, realization of the full potential of this approach will require significant research progress in several areas. In the absence of such progress, it is not clear that highly intelligent tutorial systems will be available for wide deployment within the schools for some time. Although some of the more recent work on computer-based tutorial systems may well prove useful within a constructivist framework, conventional CAI systems have historically been employed primarily for individual instruction in isolated basic skills, most often in a "drill-and-practice" mode.

The conventional approach to CAI is often embodied in network-based systems known as integrated learning systems (ILSs), which have typically incorporated computing and networking hardware, systems software, tutorial content, and student record management programs, all provided by the same vendor. As of 1990, approximately 10,000 such systems had been installed in the United States, and penetration is currently estimated at some 30 percent of all American schools. In recent years, however, many have argued that the use of new technologies to improve the efficiency of traditional instructional methods will result in limited progress at best. This view holds that the real promise of technology in education lies in its potential to facilitate fundamental, qualitative changes in the nature of teaching and learning.

While the educational research community has by no means reached consensus on the best way to educate children, a large part of that community has in recent years converged on a core set of pedagogic principles that form the basis of the constructivist paradigm. By contrast with the more traditional view of instruction as a process involving the transmission of facts from an active teacher to a passive student, constructivists believe that learning occurs through a process in which the student plays an active role in constructing the set of conceptual structures that constitute his or her own knowledge base.

Although the intellectual roots of constructivism considerably predate the current educational reform movement, contemporary constructivist thought has been strongly influenced by models of the learning process that have evolved over the past few decades within the cognitive science research community, and which differ in significant ways from those which arose within the theoretical framework of behaviorism. Constructivist theory has given rise to an approach to educational practice that places the locus of initiative and control largely within the student, who typically undertakes substantial, "authentic" tasks, presented in a realistic context, that require the self-directed application of various sorts of knowledge and skills for their successful execution. Such activities often involve student-initiated inquiries driven at least in part by the student's own curiosity, and are designed to motivate students in a more immediate way than is typical of traditional curricula based largely on the transmission of isolated facts.

Constructivist curricula often emphasize group activities designed in part to facilitate the acquisition of collaborative skills of the sort that are often required within contemporary work environments. Such group activities may offer students of varying ages and ability levels, and having different interests and prior experience, the opportunity to teach each other -- a mode of interaction that has been found to offer significant benefits to both tutor and tutee. Explicit attention is also given to the cultivation of higher-order thinking skills, including "meta-level" learning -- the acquisition of knowledge about how to learn, and how to recognize and "debug" faulty mental models.

The educational research community is unanimous and unambivalent in endorsing the principles and practice of constructivism without qualification. For example, that project-based learning techniques may be best suited to highly qualified, highly motivated teachers, and that the extensive use of these techniques by other educators may prove disappointing. Others have raised concerns about the elimination or profound de-emphasis of externally assigned, linearly sequenced instructional content, pointing out that the authors and conveyors of such content have often devoted considerable attention to the choice of a presentation order they believe is likely to facilitate understanding. While the foundations of constructivism provide a rich source of plausible and theoretically compelling hypotheses, the fact remains that the question of how best to teach children remains an empirical question that has not yet been fully answered.

Although technology is likely to find use within a number of more traditional instructional roles as well, it seems likely that the student-centered constructivist paradigm may ultimately offer the most fertile ground for the application of technology to education. In order to optimally cultivate this ground, schools will need to make changes that extend far beyond the mere installation of a network of computers. While some benefits may be obtained by using information technologies to pursue existing curricular objectives or by adding new material to an existing course, the richest harvest is likely to accrue from a fundamental restructuring -- at least at the level of the individual course, and ideally, across disciplinary boundaries as well. Such fundamental restructuring, however, is likely to prove complex, difficult, expensive, and time-consuming, and may encounter resistance from parents, educators, and the general public, particularly to the extent that such changes conflict with commonly held beliefs about the nature of knowledge and learning.

If computers are destined to play an increasingly important role in education over the next 20 years, it is natural to ask what roles will be played by human beings. Although it seems clear that the expanded use of technology in education will have significant implications for teachers, students, parents, and community members, there is reason to believe that interpersonal interactions among all these groups will be at least as important to the educational process of 2017 as they are in 1997. The use of technology within the framework of the constructivist paradigm is likely to have important implications for the day-to-day role of the teacher. When a high school student using the Internet to complete a self-directed project is able to quickly gain greater familiarity with the particular subject area in question than her teacher, for example, the teacher's traditional role as a font of knowledge is likely to become less relevant.

Because different students may be conducting different inquiries at any given point in time, this traditional role may be supplanted in part by one in which the teacher spends a considerable amount of time monitoring the activities of individual students, helping them to "debug" their emerging "mental models," and providing encouragement, direction and assistance as needed. Software can also be specifically designed to teach collaborative and cooperative skills, and to support group projects and learning exercises. In short, any fears we might have that the increasing use of computers in education will produce a generation of isolated nerds would seem to be unsupported by currently available evidence. In considering the human side of educational technology, it is also worth noting that elementary and secondary education takes place within a context that includes not only the student and teacher, but also the parents and other members of the surrounding community.

Parental and community involvement in the educational process has a significant positive effect on educational outcomes. If at least basic computing resources and Internet connectivity could be made available within the homes of those with K-12 aged children, parents would be able to receive school announcements from teachers and administrators, to communicate more easily and frequently with teachers, and to otherwise involve themselves more actively in the education of their children. The cultivation of such parental involvement may be particularly important for those students whose economic or environmental circumstances would otherwise place them at increased risk of educational failure.

There is also a growing consensus that technology should be applied in such a way as to foster broader community-wide involvement in the educational process. The linking of elementary and secondary schools with research universities, public libraries, and private companies, for example, could make valuable educational resources available to both students and teachers while simultaneously building awareness within each community of the needs of its local schools. "Real-world" projects initiated by outside organizations often generate considerable enthusiasm among students, and frequently prove unusually effective from an educational perspective. Some educators have even discussed the possibility of instituting "tele-apprenticeship" or "tele-mentoring" programs involving brief, but relatively frequent interactions between students and other community members that would be impractical in the absence of networking technologies due to travel time considerations. Conversely, high-tech schools could serve the broader community by making their computing and networking facilities available to local residents outside of school hours, or by offering state-of-the-art job training or lifelong learning programs tailored to community members, thus amortizing infrastructure costs over a larger effective user base while helping to foster intrinsically valuable community integration.

A 1992 IEA survey of school computer coordinators,found that some 41 percent of the use of computers by American K-12 students involved the acquisition of keyboarding skills; instruction in the use of word processing, database management, spreadsheet, and other software tools; and the study of computer programming. Academic subjects accounted for 54 percent of all usage at the elementary school level, but only 31 percent within the nation's high schools. At the elementary school level, computers are often employed for teaching isolated basic skills and for playing educational games. Word processing is used to a significant extent at all levels, but in most cases as part of an effort to teach computer skills, and not as a tool for writing in connection with English, social studies, or other academic classes. The situation would appear to be similar in the case of spreadsheet use, which is generally treated as an aspect of computer literacy, and less commonly integrated into, for example, the math or science curriculum.

In US among schools with access to the Internet, the most popular application is electronic mail, which is available in 93 percent of all such schools. While e-mail is generally available to administrators and teachers, however, the majority of all schools with Internet e-mail capabilities do not make this facility available to students. A majority of such schools also have access to Internet news groups, resource location applications, and World Wide Web browsers. Once again, however, such applications are more commonly accessible to teachers and administrators than to students. Little quantitative data is available at present about the frequency with which the Internet is used by the schools to access different sorts of information resources stored on remote sites.

In spite of a general appreciation of the potential for long-term growth in the market for educational software, there has thus far been only limited activity within the venture capital community aimed at launching startup companies focused on the provision of software designed for such pedagogic approaches, and targeted specifically at the nation's elementary and secondary schools. A rather long and superficially disparate list of factors has been advanced to account for the current problems within the educational software market.

If technology is to play a significant role in improving the quality of education, this figure will have to be increased very substantially. Assuming no ncrease in total spending, priorities will have to be altered to allow funds now committed to other budget categories to be redeployed—a process that is complicated in many states and school districts by various statutory and procedural constraints. In the absence of such a reallocation, software developers may not find adequate incentives to justify the substantial research and development expenditures that will be required to produce a new generation of school-based educational software products.

The market for school-based instructional software encompasses a wide range of academic subject areas (particularly at the secondary school level) and grade and skill levels. While this inherent diversity is arguably no greater (relative to the size of the potential market) than is found in various other software markets, the market for school-based educational software market (in contrast with the more robust market for home-based "edutainment" software) is further fragmented by idiosyncratic differences among the product specifications and other requirements imposed by the various states and school districts.

Since effective market size is a critical determinant of private sector investment, the limited penetration of state-of-the-art hardware has thus far impeded research and development activities that might otherwise have led to more and better educational software products. Unfortunately, this leads to a certain circularity: While software vendors are reluctant to develop products in the absence of a substantial base of modern hardware on which to run them, educators and policy-makers are reluctant to appropriate additional funds for the acquisition, maintenance, and timely replacement of hardware in the absence of a demonstrably effective base of educational software.

A substantial investment in research and development is likely to be necessary if effective educational software—and in particular, software supporting new pedagogic approaches of the sort recommended by many experts is to be made available to the schools. Economic theory predicts, however, that private firms will systematically underinvest in research and development to the extent they are unable to capture the full benefit accruing from any such activities that might ultimately prove successful. Because innovations in educational software constitute a form of intellectual property that cannot be fully appropriated by any one firm, an economically optimal level of research is likely to be conducted only in the presence of public funding at the highest level of taxing authority.

Computer-mediated Communication in Classrooms

There are various ways in which computers can support communication. In the past, this technology has been restricted to textual communication, but developments in broad bandwidth technology allow for more exciting possibilities such as synchronous shared workspaces and two-way audiovisual communication. Generally speaking, broad bandwidth is expected to afford greater opportunities for collaboration. This does mean that older technologies should be superseded. For instance, asynchronous text-based communication provides time for reflection on messages and allows students lacking in confidence to learn nevertheless by "eavesdropping" on conversations. In addition, low bandwidth communication may have some advantage in that, if it takes time and costs money in terms of connect time and if displays are restricted to a screen at a time, students may be forced to consider their responses more carefully. Computer-mediated communication settings enables the experimenter to consider the communication bandwidth as factor.

Policy makers and administrators have focused resources on improving the professional development of teachers to integrate technology into their classrooms and whole new categories of school personnel-state, district, and school instructional technology coordinators-have emerged to assist with technology planning and implementation. While students do indeed rely on the Internet to complete their schoolwork and manage their day-to-day educational activities, they say their Internet use occurs mostly outside of the school day, outside of the school building, outside of the direction of their teachers. The primary reasons for this digital disconnect between how students use the Internet for school and how schools have them use the Internet are tied to the ways that schools and teachers are oriented towards the Internet, their inability in many instances to integrate online tools into schooling, and the real and perceived barriers students face as they seek Internet access.

Internet-savvy students make clear that school leaders-more so than individual teachers-set the tone for Internet use in their classes. The differences across schools from which students were drawn are striking. Schools have different levels of access to the Internet, different requirements for student technology literacy skills, and different restrictions on student Internet access. Some of the more Internet-savvy schools offer a range of classes that require the use of the Internet-on such topics as Web site design or e-commerce-or allow students to take wholly online courses. Other schools maintain school Web sites that contain up-to-date information about the school, its schedule and events.

Some schools encourage teachers to provide their email addresses to students and their parents. And, some Internet-savvy schools even provide students with remote access over the Internet to password-protected personalized network folders and files-online access to virtual school lockers, if you will. The way that students use the Internet for school is largely driven by the kinds of activities and assignments that teachers create. The Internet is used differently by students depending on whether the use occurs inside or school or outside it. One reason for this disparity, of course, is time use. Within a typical six-hour school day, students routinely move from place to place and from teacher to teacher, from math class to lunch to gym to English class, etc. There is simply not much time within the school day for students to be sitting at Internet-connected computers. Skipping lunch to be able to access the Internet for 10 or 15 minutes during the school day was seen as an acceptable trade-off for some students who felt like they needed that little extra in-school access. That situation contrasts sharply with the online experiences of Internet-savvy students once they leave school.

Some of the heaviest Internet-using students are online several hours a day-from when they come home from school until dinner and sometimes after dinner as well. Students are simply much more in control of their time out of school than inside it. In many cases, this limited access has to do with a lack of enough Internet-connected computers-that are also in working condition-in schools and classrooms. Within a school, access to the Internet is largely controlled by teachers-teachers whom students describe as being motivated primarily by fear of what might happen if students use the Internet inappropriately. Of course, this is perhaps justified by the fact that students reported that some of them do use the Internet inappropriately at times to view adult-oriented sites, to shop while in school, to pirate and download music, etc.

In many cases, schools also prevent students from using instant messaging technologies, save their files to the school network, visit Web sites that teachers do not explicitly authorize them to visit, and-in perhaps the most extreme case we heard about-perform "right clicks" of their mouse to launch a innocuous pop-up menu within the Microsoft Windows operating system. One clear opportunity to leverage the use of the Internet for school would be for teachers to assign Internet-based homework to students. While some students report that their teachers do assign Internet-based homework, the vast majority says their teachers make no such assignments.

Student use of the Internet at school is fraught with constraints and limitations that cripple the potential it has for educational good, these students contend. Certainly, not every student with whom we spoke attends a school with large numbers of Internet-connected computers. In fact, nearly all thought it a good idea to have more Internet-connected computers at school. Even those students who attend highly wired schools describe a school environment that often discouraged their use of the Internet. They are frustrated by their inability to go online at school. Many believe that these frustrations arose because teachers do not see educational value in providing abundant Internet access, or because of fears about inappropriate material on the Internet. Students believe that professional development and technical assistance for teachers are crucial for effective integration of the Internet into curricula. Most students freely offered up numerous examples of teacher-directed uses of the Internet for school that seemed to have dubious educational value. In this regard, it is interesting to note that students are uniformly more interested in-and saw more value in-doing schoolwork that challenged and excited them than in simply using the Internet for its own sake. The students held many misconceptions about such basic things as how to use search engines, how computer viruses are contracted and spread, and how their privacy might be compromised online-just to cite a few examples. Students with better Internet skills and with greater knowledge of educational Web sites had a significant edge over other students.

Students insist that policy makers take the "digital divide" seriously and that they begin to understand the more subtle inequities among teenagers that manifest themselves in differences in the quality of student Internet access and use. The gap between students who do and don't have access to the Internet at home is a serious matter to these students. In the classroom, it is apparent to Internet-savvy students when a classmate does not have access to the Internet. Indeed, students with easy Internet access assert that they have a clear and persistent advantage over their peers with little or no access. Of course, student use of the Internet for school does not occur in a vacuum. Students' experiences, and those of their states, districts, schools, teachers, and parents, strongly affect the way the Internet is used for educational purposes. Indeed, while good schools of today are expected to have significant computer and Internet facilities, they face significant barriers to integrating it into their operations. Even when cost, technical, training and use, and equity matters have not been at issue, schools have faced legal, policy, and ethical tensions around whether and what type of access minors should have to the Internet. In such a chilled, or potentially chilled, environment, school leaders, teachers, and resource personnel have had good reason to be cautious about the kind of access they provide to students and about the extent to which they integrate the Internet into their curricula and instructional practices. The resultant Internet-use policies, filtering technologies, and human misgivings have all made adoption of the Internet challenging for educational institutions, teachers and students.

Nonetheless, students themselves are changing because of their use of and reliance on the Internet. They are coming to school with different expectations, different skills, and different resources. In fact, most Internet-savvy students told that their schools, teachers and peers are at times frustratingly illiterate, naïve, and even afraid of the online world. Indeed, students who rely on the Internet for school-who cannot conceive of not using it for their schoolwork-may ultimately force schools to change to better accommodate them. According to the students with whom we spoke, many schools have yet to react or even to recognize the changes in the ways that Internet-savvy students communicate and access information. In the midst of other priorities, schools can choose to view this emerging pressure for change from their student body in either a positive or negative light. On the positive side, through the growing use of the Internet outside of school, educators have the opportunity to expand their reach and to engage students in new and thoughtful ways. On the negative side, the sanctity and tradition of the four walls of the classroom quite literally is melting away. Students are likely to be increasingly dissatisfied with conventional approaches to teaching and learning and to the limited resources available to them in all but the best-equipped schools.

The effects of access to computers and subject-matter responsibilities on frequency of use are difficult to disentangle because access and subject-matter are related as well. That is, teachers of some subjects are much more likely to have many computers available in their own classroom than are teachers of other subjects. In particular, more than 80% of secondary teachers of computer education classes, two-thirds of business education teachers and 23% of vocational education teachers had a ratio of computers-to-students in their classroom of at least 1-to-4; that is, if they had 24 students, they had at least 6 computers. In comparison, that density of classroom computer access prevailed for only one in ten academic secondary teachers and only 5% of elementary teachers. Among the secondary academic subjects, for only English and science did a majority of teachers have any computers in their classroom. At the elementary level, a small number of computers, typically one or two, were present in the classrooms of most teachers, whether teachers of self-contained classes or subject specialists. For elementary teachers and for secondary English teachers, even small numbers of computers in their own classroom lead half of them to use computers regularly with students. For most other subjects, there has to be a substantial number of computers present for a majority of computer-assigning teachers to make computer activities a regular and frequent component of their classroom practice.

In most elementary classes, teachers see their students for much longer periods of time. As a result, they can use that extended time to orchestrate computer use among many students, even when they have only a handful of computers present. Another reason may be that given the ways that most elementary level teachers currently use computers the most significant computer use may occur in computer labs away from the classroom, so the number present in the classroom may not make so much of a difference in frequency of use. Teachers without a sufficient number of computers in their classroom generally have access to shared school or department facilities-specialized computer laboratories or more general resource areas such as a library or media centre.

Typically, computer labs and libraries accommodate many more students at one time than computer-present classrooms do. Thus, teachers with only one or two classroom computers may have their students use computers in a lab instead of using the limited number in the classroom. In sum, most teachers who use computers with their students, particularly at the secondary levels, use them in some room where there are a substantial number of computers present. Secondary teachers with just five or six computers in their classroom are much more likely to use computers on a regular basis than are teachers of the same subjects who make use of computer labs with substantially more computers in them but who have few, if any, computers in their own room. This may seem counter-intuitive since being in a lab with three times as many computers as these classrooms would seem to give individual students more opportunities to use computers. However, it seems that the computer's value in most secondary classes is not for concentrated whole-class use on a scheduled basis, but as a resource available for particular groups of students when needed to find, analyze, or communicate information.

This analysis does not take into account the economies that centralized placement of computers involve. In other words, if all of a school's two dozen academic subject-matter teachers had five computers in their classrooms instead of sharing 30 computers in a computer lab, four times as many computers in total would be required.

During most the 1990's, American schools followed the pattern of American businesses and families of moving more of students' computer work onto computers running the Windows operating system. This pattern was not uniform, however, and certain types of teachers have their students use computers with the Apple Macintosh operating system. Although the two operating systems have strong similarities, they do differ in the number of discrete instructional products available, in the learning time required to become expert in their use, and in other ways. Windows' dominance is clearest among secondary computer education teachers, business education teachers, and vocational education teachers-the groups that are most likely to assign computer work to students frequently and who have access to higher ratios of computers to students. Macintosh computers are used by almost three-quarters of fine arts teachers, and that platform also dominates the arrangements where students of "miscellaneous-subjects" academic teachers use computers in secondary schools. Among elementary school teachers, those who teach specialized programs, rather than a self-contained class, are more likely than are other elementary computer-assigning teachers to have their students use Macintosh computers.

Studies of instructional uses of school computers conducted in the 1980's and early in the 1990's found that the primary uses of computer technology in schools involved students practicing basic math and language arts skills and becoming "computer literate" (e.g., learning how to use different types of software). Today, although a large fraction of students' use of computers still occurs in special computer classes and pull-out programs, larger numbers of teachers going beyond simple skills practice or basic computer literacy and having their students use computers to do productive work-for example, searching for information and producing written and visual products that reflect their cognitive and creative effort. Of all of the various types of software available on school computers, word processing software is by far the most commonly used. Not only are English teachers, business education teachers and computer teachers more likely to have their students do word processing than any other computer activity, but so are science, social studies, vocational education, and elementary teachers.

Altogether, 50% of all 4th through 12th grade teachers have students use word processing software at least occasionally during class time. Among elementary classes, games for practicing basic math and language arts skills are still common. However in secondary schools, games are used much less frequently. In middle schools, drills and games are used by fewer teachers' students than are CD-ROM reference software or Web browsers. In high schools, drill and game software is used by fewer teachers' students than graphics software, spreadsheets, simulation and exploratory software, computer-aided presentations software (e.g., PowerPoint), CD-ROMs or web browsers. Mathematics teachers, however, appear to be an exception to this trend of using "tool-oriented" computer applications in secondary schools (except perhaps for their use of graphing calculators, which was not part of. More math teachers use skills-practice games than any other type of computer software.

In elementary school teachers' practices, the more controlled information bases on CD-ROMs are used much more often than the more wide-open information repositories on the Internet. However, in high schools the World Wide Web is used at least as often as CD-ROMs, and the Web is the information resource of choice particularly in computer-assigning foreign language classes, fine arts classes, computer classes, and business education classes. Use of analytic software-such as spreadsheets, simulations and exploratory environments-and product-oriented software-such as presentation software, graphics programs, and multimedia authoring environments-are used by fewer academic subject-matter teachers than use word processing or information retrieval software. However, computer and business education teachers are more likely to use most types of analytic and product-oriented software than they are to use information retrieval technologies like CD-ROMs and the World Wide Web. For example, two-thirds of computer teachers and business education teachers have students use spreadsheets while only about one-fourth to one-third have students use CD-ROMs. In contrast, only 19% of science teachers' students use spreadsheets, but nearly twice that number have students use CD-ROMs. More than one-third of computer and business education teachers have their students use presentation software, but that is done by only about 10% of teachers in the academic subjects.

Overall, the broadest use of different types of software occurs among computer and business education teachers, and the next broadest use is among secondary vocational education teachers, elementary teachers, and secondary teachers of mixed or other academic subjects." Those teachers are much more likely to have students use a variety of software-or any one type of software-than are more traditional "single subject" secondary teachers. Computer and business education teachers accounted for 3 more examples, involving Web use and spreadsheets. The final two examples were elementary self-contained class teachers' use of skill practice games and mixed academic secondary teachers' use of CD-ROMs. The rest of the combinations of computer use by subject involved only a small percentage of teachers. For example, among English teachers only 4% had students use presentation software on at least 10 occasions. Among science teachers, only 5% had students use simulation or modelling software that often. Among vocational teachers, only 7% had students make frequent use of spreadsheets or database software. And only 4% of math teachers had students use word processing 10 times. Outside of business and computer teachers, outside of word processing, CD-ROM use, and World Wide Web use, and outside of skill practice games in elementary school, there were almost no examples of a type of software being used frequently by more than 20% of any one category of teacher.

Most types of software have their widest diffusion in applied and elective areas of the secondary school curriculum where teachers are freer to adopt technology-based approaches to instruction. Except for word processing, CD-ROM software, and the World Wide Web, relatively few college preparatory academic teachers even experiment with simulation software, graphics software, presentation software, spreadsheets, or databases. Teachers in those subjects not only have fewer classroom computers, but they may be more constrained by expectations for subject-matter coverage against implementing teaching approaches in which computer activities are tools for student projects. As a result, one would not expect to find major outcomes of student computer use in schools by examining high school students' achievement on academic tests of mathematics skill or science or social studies knowledge. It would be more appropriate to attend to the competencies likely to be affected by the ways computers are used-primarily, given the broad use of word processing, in terms of writing competence, and in a range of applied secondary courses where teachers prepare students to be productive users of occupationally relevant technology tools and resources. Hyperstudio is used for enabling students to produce media-integrated products, while Accelerated Reader has become a highly popular system for increasing student effort in reading.

In a few secondary school subjects, one or two specialized software titles have become popular with a substantial fraction of computer-assigning teachers. Similarly, the adult-level automated drafting program, AutoCAD, was reported to be their most valuable software by nearly one-fourth of all vocational education teachers who used computers with their classes. In vocational education classes, AutoCAD plays a similar role that adult-level office software (e.g., Microsoft Office, Word Perfect, etc.) does in business education classes-as an occupational tool for which skill mastery is an explicit goal. However, the high percentage of mathematics teachers who reported Geometer's Sketchpad to be among their best software was unexpected. Most academic subject areas have many specialized software titles, causing utilization to be split among many different programs.

Computer-based teaching between teachers whose students use word-processing or skill-games and those who have students use presentation, e-mail, and multimedia software. First, these two groups of teachers may have different teaching responsibilities. Teachers of computer classes would be likely to have students use a greater variety of software than would history teachers, for example. Second, there is an order of difficulty involved in the use of different types of software. In order for their students to use presentation software or multimedia authoring software, teachers must have greater facility with having students do computer-based projects, and they may need more general expertise in the use of computers as well. Third, teachers whose students do e-mail and multimedia projects may have different objectives for computer use and different teaching philosophies than those who assign computer-based drills or word processing. For example, they may see students using computers to learn through making products or through communicating ideas to others while skill-game-using teachers and even many word-processing-assigning teachers may see computers as valuable for students to simply "do school work."

At the middle school level, there are five different clusters whose teachers provide students with a substantial variety and frequency of computer use. However, each of the five diverse-use clusters has a relatively distinct pattern in the types of software students use. Students in all five clusters make substantial use of word processing, but Cluster 2-6 is otherwise focused only on CD-ROMs and the World Wide Web, while Cluster 2-7 teachers have students use CD-ROMs, games, and simulations, but not the Web, and Cluster 2-8 teachers' students use the Web a great deal, along with more occasional use of a variety of software including spreadsheets, presentation software, and multimedia authoring. Cluster 2-9 teachers' students are particularly heavy users of presentation software, multimedia authoring, and graphics related programs for printed output, but they are not as "information"-oriented as Clusters 2-6 through 2-8. Cluster 2-10 shows the broadest pattern of software use even extending to student electronic mail.

In order to make use of all teachers' data, the percentages and rates in this section come from the full set of TLC schools-that is, both the probability sample and the various purposively selected reform-involved and high-technology schools. However, in many respects, differences among these two samples of teachers are hardly noticeable. For example, the percentage of teachers who are in clusters 2 through 10 combined is nearly the same in the probability sample as it is among the teachers in the reform-plus-high-tech TLC schools. At the secondary school levels, both middle- and high school, subject-matter responsibilities strongly affect the placement of teachers into different clusters. Three groups of middle-grades teachers are particularly likely to be in the five "diverse-use clusters"-teachers who primarily teach classes in computers, vocational education teachers, and teachers of mixed academic subjects. Those teachers are about twice as likely to be in one of the diverse-use clusters than into one of the others, "limited-use" or "specialized-use" clusters. For comparison, most of the single-subject academic teachers are split about evenly between limited- or specialized-use clusters and diverse-use clusters. The most sharply distinctive pattern is held by computer-assigning middle grades mathematics teachers. Those teachers are five times as likely to be in the limited- or specialized-use clusters as in the diverse-use clusters.

In high schools, the most active computer-assigning teachers also fall into five clusters. As with the more diverse-use clusters at the middle school level, relatively few teachers belong to these upper-end clusters. Altogether, for example, only 6% of high school teachers comprise Clusters 3-8 through 3-10, and only 9% additionally comprise Clusters 3-6 and 3-7. One of these high-use clusters is focused on the traditional computer literacy applications of instruction in word processing, spreadsheet, and database software-and almost nothing else. Another cluster is heavily Internet-dominated, involving not only substantial use of the Web, but substantial student use of electronic mail as well. The teachers in this cluster come primarily from academic subjects, most commonly English. In this group, comparatively few teachers report that typical students in the classroom have used computers more than 40 days (twice/weekly) during the year. This may have to do with having a limited number of convenient Internet connections and e-mail accounts, since at the time of this study few academic classrooms had high-speed Internet connections and few schools provided e-mail accounts to students on locally-controlled servers. The other three high-use high school clusters are characterized by substantial use of both word processing and presentation software-in other words, both writing and speaking. Cluster 3-8 involves courses that are information-oriented; both CD-ROM reference software and World Wide Web browsers accompany the word processing and Powerpoint (presentation) activities. Like the previous cluster, 3-7, it is also primarily drawn from teachers of academic subjects, and, again, English teachers are most prevalent. In contrast, Clusters 3-9 and 3-10 are primarily populated by teachers of computer classes and business education classes.

Both involve the frequent use of several types of software in addition to word processing and presentation software, with most other types of software used occasionally as well. For Cluster 3-9, the most-used software includes spreadsheets and Web browsers. For Cluster 3-10, it includes spreadsheets, simulations, and graphics-oriented print programs. At this point, it is hard to see what distinguishes these final two clusters. However, one cluster is heavily drawn from teachers whose computer access is in their own classroom, while the other cluster overwhelmingly uses computer labs. One cluster's teachers teach students who are high in overall academic achievement and teach in high socio-economic status communities; the other's students are slightly below average in academic achievement and come from lower than average socio-economic backgrounds. At each school level, some clusters are characterized by the use of one particular type of software with students, if not exclusively then at least far more than any other type. Cluster 1-2 at the elementary level, whose students experience computers primarily through word processing. Cluster 2-2 is similar at the middle school level, except that CD-ROMs and graphics-oriented printing substitute for games as a secondary computer activity. Cluster 3-5 is comparable for high school teachers except that these teachers also have their students use the World Wide Web and/or CD-ROMs. English teachers and science teachers constitute the largest fraction of teachers who fit the "primarily word-processing" Clusters 2-2 and 3-5. Math teachers constitute nearly one-half (47%) of the teachers in middle school

Cluster 2-3, in which skill-based games are the dominant mode of computer activity, supported by simulations and limited spreadsheet or database work.

Industrial arts and fine arts teachers together are the majority of teachers in high school Cluster 3-3, whose teachers report very frequent use of graphics software (CAD in industrial arts, varied drawing and design software in fine arts) along with word processing software as well. High school science teachers are one-third of the teachers in Cluster 3-4, where use focuses on World Wide Web browser programs like Netscape, along with some CD-ROM reference software. Interestingly enough, very little word processing is done in those classes. A somewhat similar cluster, 2-5, is formed at the middle school level by teachers from a wide range of subjects whose students use Web browser software supported by word processing. Although the teachers in these "specialized-use" clusters have students use a less varied array of software, many of them make computers a part of their classes' instructional activities. Overall, about 25% of the teachers in these clusters have had their "typical student" use computers on more than 40 occasions during the year. Thus, another way of classifying teachers would be to create categories based on both extent of student computer use and variety of software used.

Several other aspects of teachers' computer use-the objectives they have for students' use, their students' use of computers outside of class, the extent to which they use computers themselves professionally, and their self-perceived expertise in using computers-we will provide a richer portrait of many of these software-use clusters. Not only is there a wide variety of different kinds of software that teachers can use with students, but most types of software can be used for different instructional purposes by different teachers. For example, one teacher may have students do word processing in order to improve how well they communicate their ideas, while another teacher may have students use the same software so they can become more proficient in basic grammar, and another may have students do word processing in pairs or triplets in order for them to learn to work more collaboratively. In other words, the use of computers to have students learn content knowledge and to improve their writing has taken over from the "computer literacy" and "skills practice" objectives that dominated students' teacher-directed computer use during the 1970s and 1980s. This suggests that teachers are now seeing computers as advantageous for somewhat more complex competencies than the role they assigned to computers heretofore. Even among elementary teachers, the writing and information-acquisition objectives were more common than the skills objectives.

In fact, a higher percentage of elementary computer-assigning teachers than secondary teachers named "writing" as a principal objective. Still, elementary teachers were also more likely than teachers at other levels were to report that "remediation of skills not learned well" and "computer skills" were among their top three objectives for computer use. In contrast, computer-assigning teachers of older children were more likely to point to objectives such as having students analyze information and present it to others as a main reason for using computers. Some of the differences are self-evident-for example, that English teachers are more likely than other teacher s to use computers to help students improve their writing, or that computer teachers are more apt than others to have "improving computer skills" as a principal objective. However, other patterns of objectives chosen in response to this survey question suggest that different pedagogical perspectives may characterize teachers of different subjects. Foreign language teachers, for example, were much less likely than others to select "learning to work collaboratively," while math teachers were the least likely to see computers as useful for having students communicate electronically with other people. Teachers have widely varying objectives for students' use of computers according to the subject-matter that they teach. For example, 82% of business education teachers report that reinforcing skill acquisition is one of their top three objectives, compared to only 20% of social studies teachers.

One key finding is that academic skills-related objectives such as reinforcement or remediation are associated with greater use of the software category "games for practicing skills" and less use of everything else. This is consistent with the earlier finding that many teachers who use skill games software such as teachers in Cluster 2-3, are less likely to use other types of software. Teachers who prioritize student written expression using computers also make use of CD-ROMs more than other teachers do. Teachers who prioritize having students use computers to present information to an audience not only are more likely than others to use presentation software, but they are also the primary leaders in student use of multimedia authoring software such as Hyperstudio. Thirty percent of such teachers use multimedia authoring software with their students compared to 10% of all other computer-assigning teachers. Looking at this from the opposite perspective, 39% of multimedia-authoring software users selected "presenting information to an audience" as a primary objective of student computer use compared to 15% of all other computer-assigning teachers.

Although teachers may have their most direct effects on students' learning during class time, teachers also affect how much effort students take to do school work at other times-before and after school and at other times away from the school building. Teachers who reported that students did out-of-class-time computer work differ from other teachers in terms of which subjects they taught, the overall level of student achievement in their class, the socio-economic level of the school's population, and according to which objectives they had for student computer use. Thus, student characteristics, teaching responsibilities, and approach to computer use all affect the likelihood that students will supplement their in-class computer work with time before or after school or at home, at least as measured by teacher surveys. In terms of subject-matter, two-fifths of all science teachers who assign computer work during class reported that most or all students did computer work at school outside of class time. On the other hand, only 10% of computer-assigning math teachers did. Other secondary teachers with higher-than-average rates of reporting before- and after-school computer use included teachers of computer classes and social studies teachers. Besides math teachers, three other groups of teachers reported limited out-of-class-time computer work by students-vocational education teachers, business education teachers, and elementary teachers of self-contained classes. With respect to students using computers to do work for the class at home, more computer-assigning English teachers reported students doing this than any other group of teachers.

Science and foreign language teachers were also above-average in this regard, also suggesting that word processing is the dominant school-related use of computers at students' homes. The computer-assigning teachers least likely to report most students engaged in away-from-school computer use for class-related work were fine arts teachers (none of them did), math teachers, and vocational education teachers. For math teachers, this appears to be the continuation of the relatively low involvement of math teachers in computer work. It should be noted that while a majority fine arts and vocational education teachers reported some student computer use outside of school, 71% of computer-assigning secondary math teachers reported no outside-of-school use by students for math class at all. In the same way that teachers' objectives for student computer work affect the types of software they have students use, so, too, do those objectives appear to affect the likelihood that students will do computer work outside of class time, at school or at home.

For this analysis, combine the "out-of-class" and the "at home, out-of-school" measure and report the overall difference in the extent of participation by students in doing computer work for the class at non-class times between teachers who include each teaching objective among their three most important objectives and teachers who do not include that objective. Teachers with four objectives for their students' computer use are distinctly more likely to report higher levels of student participation in out-of-class computer work done for the class. In contrast, three groups of teachers are much less likely than other teachers to report students using computers out-of-class: those whose objectives are reinforcement of skills, remediation, and students "learning to work independently." It is interesting that teachers who value computers to help students to work independently are much less likely than others to report students actually using computers outside of their own presence! It seems plausible that for many teachers, having students "work independently" means that they prefer students to be working quietly, not that they really want them to do independent work! Teachers' objectives, as we have seen, tend to be accomplished by having students use specific types of software. Thus, it is not surprising that teachers who report their classes frequently using certain types of software are the same teachers who report the highest levels of participation in computer work being done outside of class time.

In particular, across all school levels, the teachers reporting the most out-of-class and out-of-school participation in computer activities for their classes are those who have students frequently use four types of programs: presentation software, electronic mail, multimedia authoring programs, and word processing. The high effect size for word processing is doubtlessly due to the ease with which that type of software carries over to non-supervised computer time. The equally strong relationship with out-of-class computer work for the other types of software seems more likely due to the greater engagement produced by the kinds of classroom assignments into which those types of software are incorporated.

Online Learning: Emerging Trends

Online is the perfect place to blend interaction, information, group learning, tailored learning and quality learning resources. It is inexpensive, globally contestable and there are some things which cannot be done any other way at an affordable cost. For some kinds of learning, online is unquestionably superior. It enables a larger market to be reached, but large classes are not needed. Several online groups recruit their tutors from around the world. The following are aspects of learning which can only be achieved through online:

— heavy use of colour;

— simulations, with animation and sound;

— group problem solving over distance;

— automated quizzes and essay marking;

— tailored learning paths;

— integration with online information resources.

These can be matched and manipulated online, but not in print. New forms of communication depend upon this. Colour is free online, but expensive in print. There is also some automated English essay marking taking place with considerably enhanced efficiency. The components of circuit boards can be "blown" at will in online simulations at no cost to the institution. Such simulations are free now - in future they will be sold via institutional licenses to students at low cost. Therefore, new learning processes employ various types of tools. For the first three or four months tutors are harassed electronically, then the mode shifts to student-student communication and direct student interrogation. The academic becomes a manager of learning processes to a far greater extent. The following are key guidelines for the introduction and development of online learning:

— apply formal project management techniques, or it will get out of hand;

— be creative, don't simply convert a traditional curriculum;

— mix and match traditional and online components;

— integrate rich online sources with the course;

— use appropriate expertise

— build in student evaluation.

Following are key factors in implementation:

— base it on corporate strategy;

— set up a process, do not do everything from scratch;

— write a business plan;

— get some strong partners;

— when online is the way to reach a market, use traditional marketing techniques.

Net-oriented Collborative Learning

Distributed artificial intelligence (DAI) has focused more on cooperative problem solving than on collaborative learning. While psychologists consider that learning and problem solving are similar processes, computer scientists still address them separately. Different research communities (DAI versus machine learning, for example) have developed different techniques, some for learning and some for problem solving. The 'collaboration' versus 'cooperation' is more complex. Some people use these terms interchangeably. Collaboration is distinguished from "cooperation" in that cooperative work. Its accomplished by the division of labor among participants, as an activity where each person is responsible for a portion of the problem solving, whereas collaboration involves the mutual engagement of participants in a coordinated effort to solve the problem together. Defining collaboration by the non-distribution of labour does not avoid ambiguities.

Some spontaneous division of labour may occur in collaboration. The person who has more to say about the current topic takes the task-doer's role, while the other becomes an observer, monitoring the situation. The observer can contribute by criticising and giving topic-divergent motions, which are not the primary roles of the task-doer. This distribution of roles depends on the nature of the task and may change frequently. For example, in computer-supported tasks, the participant who controls the mouse tends to be "executor", while the other is likely to be the "reflector". Cooperation and collaboration do not differ in terms of whether or not the task is distributed, but by virtue of the way in which it is divided: in cooperation, the task is split (hierarchically) into independent subtasks; in collaboration, cognitive processes may be (heterarchically) divided into intertwined layers.

The nature of collaborative learning as comprising two relatively independent cognitive systems which exchange messages. It can also be viewed as a single cognitive system with is own properties. These two different answers to the question serve to anchor the two ends of the theoretical axis. At one end, the unit of analysis is the individual. The challenge is to understand how these cognitive systems merge to produce a shared understanding of the problem. Along this axis, between the 'individual' and the 'group', we can find three different theoretical positions: socio-constructivist, socio-cultural and shared (or distributed) cognition approaches.

Moreover, for the sake of exposition, the approaches will be presented as more different than they actually are. The socio-constructivist approach enhanced the role of interactions with others rather than actions themselves.

Despite this theoretical claim, which suggests a complex intertwining between the social and the individual plane, the experimental paradigm used by its proponents involved two supposedly "individual" phases (pre- and post-test), separated by an intervention session in which subjects worked either alone or in pairs. Evidence showed that, under certain conditions, peer interaction produced superior performances on individual post-test than individual training. The studies which established this tradition of research involved children in the age-range 5-7 years, and relied essentially on Piagetian conservation tasks. Where working in pairs facilitated subsequent individual performance, the mediating process was characterised as "socio-cognitive conflict", i.e. conflict between different answers based on different centrations, embodied socially in the differing perspectives of the two subjects.

The social dimension of the situation was seen as providing the impetus towards or catalyst for resolving the conflict. Such resolution could be achieved by transcending the different centrations to arrive at a more advanced "decentred" solution. The success of the concept of conflict in computer systems is not surprising. This logical concept can be modelled in terms of knowledge or beliefs and integrated in truth maintenance systems or dialogue models. However, the main proponents of socio-cultural theory now admit that their view has probably been too mechanistic. While the socio-cognitive approach focused on individual development in the context of social interaction, the socio-cultural approach focuses on the causal relationship between social interaction and individual cognitive change. The basic unit of analysis is social activity, from which individual mental functioning develops.

A simple computational model of internalisation has been developed. The system includes two agents able to argue with each other. The agent's reasoning is implemented as an argumentation with itself. Each learner stores the conversations conducted during collaborative problem solving and re-instantiates elements from the dialogue for its own reasoning. The learner may for instance discard an argument that has been previously refuted by its partner in a similar context. The psychological reality is of course more complex, what takes place at the inter-psychological level is not merely copied to the intra-psychological, but involves an active transformation by the individual. The mechanism through which participation in joint problem solving may change the understanding of a problem is referred to as "appropriation".

As in political structures, there exist centralised systems where control is achieved by a super-agent or a central data structure (e.g., blackboard architectures) and decentralised systems in which each agent has more autonomy. An agent is more autonomous if it executes local functions without interference with external operations (execution autonomy), if it chooses when and with whom it communicates (communication autonomy) and whether it self-organises into hierarchical, serial or parallel sub-processes. The concept of shared cognition is deeply intertwined with the 'situated cognition' theory.

The environment is an integral part of cognitive activity, and not merely a set of circumstances in which context-independent cognitive processes are performed. The environment includes a physical context and a social context. Under the influence of sociologists and anthropologists, the focus is placed largely on the social context, i.e. not only the temporary group of collaborators, but the social communities in which these collaborators participate. This approach offers a new perspective on the socio-cognitive and the socio-cultural approaches, and has recently led to certain revisions by erstwhile proponents of the earlier theories. Collaboration is viewed as the process of building and maintaining a shared conception of a problem. While the previous approaches were concerned with the inter-individual plane, the shared cognition approach focuses on the social plane, where emergent conceptions are analysed as a group product. For instance, it has been observed that providing explanations leads to improve knowledge.

In the socio-cognitive perspective, the methodology was to set up conditions hypothesised to facilitate learning and to compare the outcomes of this intervention with some control group. With such methods, collaboration is treated as a black box; the focus is on outcomes. In contrast, research from a socio-cultural point of view tends to employ micro genetic analyses of the social interaction. The focus is on the processes involved in social interaction. This is partly because of the importance attached to the concept of mediation in socio-cultural theory. Evidence is sought from dialogue for symbols and concepts which mediate social activity and which can in turn be subsequently found to mediate individual activity. The shared cognition approach obviously also favours the second methodology. The choice of the dependent measures varied according to what the investigators meant by 'more efficient'. The most frequent measure was the subject's performance when solving alone the task they previously solved with somebody else.

Some researchers decomposed this dependent variable into several other measures of performance, such as the improvement of monitoring and regulation skills or a decrease in the confirmation bias. Within this paradigm, the precise analysis of effects is the only way to understand the mechanisms that make collaborative learning efficient. Nevertheless, negative results cannot always be discarded as the result of experimental errors or noise. Some negative effects are stable and well documented, for instance the fact that low achievers progressively become passive when collaborating with high achievers. There is a simple way to understand the controversial effects observed with the first paradigm: collaboration is in itself neither efficient or inefficient. Collaboration works under some conditions, and it is the aim of research to determine the conditions under which collaborative learning is efficient.

To determine the conditions under which collaborative learning is efficient, one has to vary these conditions systematically. While the first experimental approach (in very general terms) varies only in terms of the dependent measures, the second experimental approach varies along two dimensions, both dependent and independent variables. Numerous independent variables have been studied. They concern the composition of the group, the features of the task, the context of collaboration and the medium available for communication. The composition of the group covers several other independent variables such as the number of members, their gender and the differences between participants. It is not possible here to give a complete overview of the findings concerning each of these variables. Group heterogeneity is probably the most studied variable. Scholars have considered differences with respect to general intellectual development, social status or domain expertise. They have considered objective and subjective differences in expertise.

For the socio-constructivist, this difference provides the conditions for generating socio-cognitive conflict. For the socio-cultural approach, it provides conditions for internalisation. However, the nature of differences differs within each theoretical approach. Socio-cognitive theory refers to symmetrical pairs (i.e., symmetrical with respect to general intellectual or developmental level) where members have different viewpoints, whilst socio-cultural theory is concerned with asymmetric pairs where members have different levels of skill. The pressure to conform in the presence of someone with higher perceived status is not likely, in this view, to lead to genuine cognitive change. Researchers have attempted to determine the optimal degree of differences. If it is too small, it may fail to trigger interactions. If the difference is too large, there may be not interaction at all.

According Piaget, for a conflictual interaction to give rise to progress, it must prompt individual cognitive restructuring. This implies that a resolution of conflict which would be exclusively based on social regulations (compliance from one partner for instance) would prevent interaction from being efficient. Piaget's theory predicts that pre-operational children lack the ability to decentre from their own perspective and therefore benefit from collaborative work. Indeed, as others have noted, Piagetian theory in this respect leads to something of a paradox. It is not clear whether social interaction leads to the decentration necessary to benefit from collaboration, or that decentration has to happen before genuine collaboration can take place. Some research suggests that developmental factors need to be taken into account in resolving this issue.

However, with more complex tasks, which demand reasoning using that knowledge to predict the partner's actions on the basis of their belief and intentions may not be achievable until about 6 years. In order to achieve shared understanding in a collaborative activity, the child must also be able to coordinate all these representations and have sufficient skills to communicate with respect to them. Research on peer tutoring has identified some conditions which are also relevant to collaborative learning. The first condition is that the child-tutor must be skilled at the task. A second pre-requisite is the ability of the child to reflect upon his or her own performance with respect to the task. Thirdly, in order to tutor contingently (i.e., to monitor the effects of previous help on subsequent actions by the learner), the child has to be able to assess whether the learner's action was wrong with respect to the instructions or wrong with respect to the task, and then be able to produce the next tutorial action on the basis of both a representation of the previous instruction and an evaluation of the learner's response to that instruction.

In contrast, the implication from socio-cognitive theory is that tasks should promote differences in perspectives or solutions. Typically, conservation and coordination tasks involve perspective-taking, planning and problem solving. There is thus little overlap in the nature of tasks investigated from the Piagetian and Vygotskian perspective. It is also clear that the nature of the task influences the results: one cannot observe conceptual change if the task is purely procedural and does not involve much understanding; reciprocally one cannot observe an improvement of regulation skills if the task requires no planning. Some tasks are less "shareable" than others. For instance, solving anagrams can hardly be done collaboratively because it involves perceptual processes which are not easy to verbalise (if they are open to introspection at all). In contrast, some tasks are inherently distributed, either geographically (e.g., two radar-agents, receiving different data about the same aeroplane), functionally (e.g., the pilot and the air traffic controller) or temporally (e.g., the takeoff agent and the landing-agent).

Adult-child interaction may be more controlled by the adult rather than being a reciprocal relationship. Children are more likely to justify their assertions with peers than with adults. The differences between socio-cognitive and socio-cultural approaches with respect to composition of dyads are reconcilable. Tutoring or guidance may be necessary for the former, whilst collaboration between peers of equivalent intellectual ability may be better in fostering the latter. So, how dyads or groups should be composed with respect to skills and abilities may depend upon what learning outcomes one is interested in and what tasks are involved. Although few studies have involved a direct comparison of peer collaboration and peer tutoring with the same task, the type of task may interact with the developmental level of the learner and the nature of the dyad.

The complexity of the findings collected in the second paradigm led to the emergence of a third one. This introduces intermediate variables that describe the interactions that occur during collaboration. The question "under which conditions is collaborative learning efficient?" is split into two (hopefully simpler) sub-questions: which interactions occur under which conditions and what effects do these interactions have. The key is to find relevant intermediate variables, i.e., variables that describe the interactions and that can be empirically and theoretically related to the conditions of learning and to learning outcomes. Rogoff conducted various experiments in which children solved a spatial planning task with adults or with more skilled peers. She measured the performance of children in a post-test performed without help. Overall she found better results with adult-child than with child-child pairs but, more interestingly, she identified an intermediate variable which explains these variations. Effective adults involved the child in an explicit decision making process, while skilled peers tended to dominate the decision making.

This was confirmed by the children who collaborated with an adult; those who scored better in the post-test were those for which the adults made the problem solving strategy explicit. These results are slightly biased by the fact that the proposed task (planning) is typically a task in which metaknowledge plays the central role. A socio-cultural interpretation would be that the explication of the problem solving strategy provides the opportunity to observe and potentially internalise the partner's strategy. From a socially shared cognition viewpoint, one could say that making the strategy explicit is the only way to participate in each other's strategy and progressively establish a joint strategy. When collaboration is mediated via a computer system, the design of this system impacts on the collaborative process. This mediation has methodological advantages: the experimenter may have explicit control over some aspects of collaboration (e.g., setting rules for turn taking, determining the division of labour or distribution of activities).

The effects of the computer as medium also has pedagogical aspects: to support the type of interactions that are expected to promote learning. There are three settings in which the computer influences collaboration. Two human users collaborate on a computer-based task Until relatively recently, one of the main advantages associated with computer use in schools was seen in terms of the potential for individualised learning. However, since schools generally have more students than computers, children often work in groups at the computer. Several empirical results suggest that group work - at least dyadic work - at the computer may enhance the benefit derived from the collaborative learning situation. The specific questions to be addressed here deal with the extent to which learner(s)-computer interaction and human-human interaction can reciprocally enhance one another. For instance, interfaces which induce a specific distribution of roles between learning partners help to foster social interaction. Such interfaces can serve to scaffold the executive and regulative aspects of the collaborative task.

Another interesting example concerns the principle of immediate feedback which was seen as a critical feature in the first generation of educational software. In other words, aspects of the software can modify the socio-cognitive dynamics between the learning partners. In particular, the computerised learning environment constitutes in itself a mediational resource which can contribute to create a shared referent between the social partners. Different interfaces, different computer-based tasks and activities may yield very different interactions and learning outcomes. However, for the sake of simplicity, refer generically to computer-based activities in order to discuss the other general parameters which exert an influence (e.g., frequency of feedback, representations induced by the interface, role distribution, etc.).

Training for Teachers

As schools continue to acquire more and better hardware and software, the benefit to students increasingly will depend on the skill with which some three million teachers are able to use these new tools. In order to make effective use of educational technology, teachers will have to master a variety of powerful tools, redesign their lesson plans around technology-enhanced resources, solve the logistical problem of how to teach a class full of students with a smaller number of computers, and take on a complex new role in the technologically transformed classroom. Yet teachers currently receive little technical, pedagogic or administrative support for these fundamental changes, and few colleges of education adequately prepare their graduates to use information technologies in their teaching.

As a result, most teachers are left largely on their own as they struggle to integrate technology into their curricula. Moreover, when teachers do make use of information technologies, they are often used for either teaching students about computers or for drill and practice sessions focusing on the acquisition of isolated basic skills. Most teachers report that computers initially make their job more difficult. Despite the daunting challenge of using computers and networks appropriately within an educational context, however, teachers commonly report that they have not received adequate preparation in the effective use of computers within the classroom. Part of the problem arises from the fact that school districts frequently purchase hardware and software without allocating sufficient funds to help teachers learn to use the new equipment within an educational context.

Teachers often have a negative reaction to the narrowly technical orientation of most technology-related courses, which show them how to operate a computer, but not how to use computers to enhance their teaching. Returning to the classroom from what are typically semi-annual encounters with such courses, they are generally unprepared to handle the diverse logistical and curricular challenges they encounter within a technology-rich environment. In the Panel's view, what teachers actually need is in-depth, sustained assistance as they work to integrate computer use into the curriculum and confront the tension between traditional methods of instruction and new pedagogic methods that make extensive use of technology. Such assistance should include not only purely technical support, but pedagogic support as well, ideally including observation within the classrooms of successful technology-using teachers, periodic consultation with more experienced mentors, and ongoing communication with other teachers grappling with similar challenges. Less than five percent of all schools, however, have such a full-time professional on staff.

However, most teachers cannot use computers effectively unless someone is available to help not only with the technical problems that are likely to arise from time to time, but also with the deeper pedagogic challenges of choosing software, organizing projects that make use of technology, and learning how to guide students in the use of computer-based resources. If a school cannot afford to hire a full-time technology coordinator to assist its teachers, it may be possible to provide adequate (though perhaps suboptimal) technical and pedagogic support at the district level.

The provision of training and assistance will take time away from the other responsibilities of these teachers—an implicit cost that should be realistically assessed in comparing the alternatives for providing technological support to the rest of the faculty. Cause for optimism, however, may be found in certain contributions that technology itself may ultimately make to the development of expertise in the educational applications of computers and networks. Information technology may also help teachers to recover at least some of the time they have invested in deploying technology on behalf of their students. Some types of educational software, for example, may ultimately enable students to spend part of the school day learning with less continuous attention from a teacher.

Online seminars conducted over the Internet might prepare teachers to use technology at roughly half the cost of conventional courses for which the teachers must be physically present, and equally important, might make it feasible to provide opportunities for followup consultation and mentoring on an ongoing basis without the prohibitive travel expenses that would be associated with repeated face-to-face meetings.

The Internet also provides an excellent medium for various forms of communication among teachers themselves, including the sharing not only of ideas, but of actual lesson plans and curricular materials as well. If teachers were given adequate instruction in the art of computer-enhanced pedagogy and had access to on-site assistance as needed, they would be in a better position to reap the benefits of educational technology, but one major obstacle would remain: a lack of sufficient time in their schedules to become familiar with available hardware, software, and content; to prepare technology-related material for use in the classroom; and to share ideas on technology use with other teachers.

In US over 200,000 new teachers enter the profession each year, and there is a 50 percent turnover in the teaching force approximately every 15 years. While advances in underlying technologies, educational software, and pedagogic methods will result in an ongoing need for in-service training, colleges of education have a valuable opportunity to introduce future teachers to the use of educational technology before the demands of an actual teaching position begin to impinge on the time available for such training. Judging solely from teacher certification requirements in the various states, it would at first appear that education students receive more technology-related instruction than do active teachers: Eighteen states require pre-service technology training, while only two require in-service technology training. Pre-service requirements, however, can typically be satisfied by completing a course on how to operate a computer, or by taking a "methods" course in which educational technology is discussed, but never actually used by either the professor or the students.

As a result, even in states with a technology-related certification requirement, new teachers typically graduate with no experience in using computers to teach, and little knowledge of available software and content. Colleges of education fail to instruct their students in the use of educational technology for reasons that mirror some of the major obstacles to the spread of technology at the K-12 level, including the inadequate allocation of funds for hardware and software, minimal technology-related professional development for the education school faculty, and a lack of time for professors of education to restructure their courses. Education schools generally have the advantage of better technical support (often provided through the campus computer center) than elementary and secondary schools, but research, publishing, and other academic responsibilities place additional demands on the faculty, thus slowing the process of curricular reform.

If the promise of educational technology is to be realized, educators and policy-makers will thus unavoidably be faced with difficult decisions as they attempt to either control or justify a secular trend of increasing (inflation-adjusted) per capita educational spending within the constraints imposed by a number of well-entrenched claimants on current financial resources. The potential role of technology in increasing educational productivity, it is worth noting that teachers are likely to play a critically important role within the sort of future classroom envisioned by most current researchers in the field of educational technology. While this may be a comfort to fearful teachers, it may also be a disappointment to those who have looked to technology for a simplistic automation of the instructional function, accompanied by a wholesale reduction in nation's aggregate expenditures on teacher compensation. The empirical validation of such an analysis is complicated by the fact that the return on an educational investment is determined in large part by such factors as lifetime earnings, along with a number of non-pecuniary factors even less amenable to straightforward quantification.

However, it seems quite possible that in the presence of formidable global economic competition, a substantial nationwide investment in educational technology could be justified even if no value were placed on the direct benefits accruing to the people, using return calculations based solely on the additional tax revenues associated with an increase in their expected lifetime taxable earnings. Equitable access to information technologies in education has been a central concern of educators and policy-makers since microcomputers first entered nation's schools some twenty years ago, but has gained special attention during a period in which powerful desktop computers and global Internet connectivity are rapidly becoming an integral part of our daily lives.

It has been frequently noted that new computing and networking technologies have the potential to empower historically disadvantaged groups with greater access to the sorts of knowledge-building and communication tools that might help them to overcome at least some of their respective disadvantages. This potential can scarcely be overstated, it also believes that the ways in which educational technologies are actually deployed and used will determine whether they serve to narrow these historical disparities or widen them even further. The current accessibility of computing and networking technologies to various segments of student population is then reviewed, with special attention to differences associated with socioeconomic status, race and ethnicity, geographical factors, gender, and various types of special student needs.

Schools with higher computer densities typically provide greater access to other forms of educational technology (including local- and wide-area networks and peripherals supporting multimedia applications) as well, making computer density a useful (albeit imperfect) proxy for the level of overall technology deployment. While the ratio of computers to students varies widely from school to school, and while much of this variation is accounted for by other factors.

Poorer schools may have fewer teachers capable of making effective use of educational technologies, thus limiting both the quality and quantity of computer use by their students. The most significant disparities in access to technology, however, are currently found not in the schools, but in the homes of their students. Consideration should also be given to the provision of various forms of private sector incentives for the expeditious wiring of impoverished rural and inner city schools to support local- and wide-area networking.

Motivation for technology teachers

The content, instructional methodologies, and facilities are among the key indicators of change as is the background and motivation of people who choose to become technology teachers. Individuals interested in computers and electronic communication are seeking technology teaching positions, as contrasted with interests in woodworking and metalworking that typified the past. The profession could benefit from information about how these changes have affected teachers' enjoyment of teaching. This information could inform the process of recruiting new teachers by better understanding the rewards and stresses associated with major programmatic change.

Technology education is having difficulty recruiting talented teachers. Current estimates place the number of job openings at six or more for each technology education baccalaureate graduate. Attractive salary and benefit packages accompany many of these openings. Research has established a relationship between teacher satisfaction and student achievement. The findings indicate that secondary school teacher morale depends in part on whether their students were relatively high scholastic achievers. Similarly, student achievement tended to increase as a function of high teacher morale.

Teacher morale or satisfaction may be one of the most important factors affecting student achievement, and therefore, is a critical topic to be researched. The literature on teacher satisfaction indicates that job satisfaction is the result of many interrelated factors. Studies of teacher satisfaction based on Maslow's hierarchy of needs theory have supported the connection between need-fulfilment and job satisfaction. These authors cited an absence of three higher-order needs (esteem, autonomy, and self-actualisation) as major contributors to low teacher satisfaction. Simmons has identified teacher satisfaction factors and has categorised them as *content* and *context*. Content factors relate to the teaching process itself (e.g., achievement in teaching, the nature of the work itself, and recognition), while context factors relate to the job situation (e.g., interpersonal relations, school policy, salary, etc.). The context serves only to reduce pain in the lower-order needs areas (e.g., physiological and safety) and cannot lead to satisfaction. The content aspects correspond to esteem and self-actualisation, which are at the top of Maslow's hierarchy. Those factors that are *content*-centered (i.e., intrinsic aspects of teaching) contribute most powerfully to satisfaction.

Teacher satisfaction was not significantly affected by background variables such as teacher or principal gender, years of experience, or school-type assignment. Teachers' perception of locus of control is another factor influencing job satisfaction. There is no predominant reason that teachers cite for leaving teaching. Among the reasons are salary, limited opportunities for advancement, and too much to do in too little time. Furthermore, factors such as low salary, low status, and excessive paperwork were found to be major sources of stress among teachers.

However, the intention to leave teaching was more related to their coping resources. Common reasons for leaving included problems with student discipline, lack of student motivation, and lack of respect from community, parents, administrators, and students.

The two primary reasons that these teachers like teaching technology is the excitement and stimulation of learning and working with new technologies, as well as the enjoyment of working with students. These teachers desire and receive a fair degree of autonomy in their daily jobs with regard to developing and implementing curriculum. The teachers in this study find the lack of funding and equipment, the decline in the personal characteristics of some students, and the lack of understanding and support of administrators and counsellors to be the most frustrating aspects of their jobs. The overwhelming majority of the suggestions offered by the outstanding teachers may be summarised in two broad categories:

1) better funding and support for technology education, and

2) educating the public about technology education.

Technology education professionals or their associations cannot directly address issues such as better funding for schools/teachers or issues related to student discipline. However, the profession can appropriately address the major misconceptions regarding technology education and enlist the support of business and industry in doing so. This may help alleviate the two major concerns expressed by the teachers.

Some teachers have warmly welcomed the challenge of introducing technology education to children at an early age. They have found that it has allowed them to develop new dimensions to work already underway. For others the idea has been received with more caution, for a variety of reasons. Some are confused by what technology education would mean for young children. Others are concerned that limited resources would be stretched too thinly if the younger age group were included and that the primary curriculum is already overloaded. There are also those who believe that technology education is simply inappropriate with a younger age group. Expanding the technology curriculum to primary schools raises a number of important issues. Any developments should be based on sound educational principles and thinking. Following are the key considerations:

i) the value of including technology in the curriculum for young children;

ii) critical dimensions to nurturing technological capability;

iii) appropriate models of teaching, learning and assessing;

vi) addressing the needs of the teacher; and

v) the importance of providing coherent, progressive and continuous technological experiences.

Technological capability is dependent on the ability to take action, to intervene in the made world, and to create new or improved products or systems. The children who are given more support to find out how things work, to make things work, and to create and to express themselves, the better chance there is for their technological capability to prosper. Children in the first years of life will encounter a wide variety of experiences. For some there will be an abundance of opportunities to develop confidence and skill in those aspects that support technological capability. For others the opportunities will be limited.

The range of experiences will be affected by a number of economic, social, cultural and philosophical influences and these in turn will impact on the way in which capability develops. There are, for example, indications of the effect that gender based expectations have on the early technological experiences of girls and boys and the consequences this has for children's development. A main function of formal schooling is to take control over the experiences children have and to attempt to provide some equity in opportunities.

If we accept that technology is an inherently important dimension of a child's curriculum, there is a logic to proposing that the earlier we, as educationalists, involve ourselves in this aspect of development, the better. Leaving this to chance, or at least until children enter secondary schooling seems a little haphazardous if not dangerous. But introducing technology into the curriculum of young children is also important because of the propensity of this age group to engage in technological activity with an enthusiasm, curiosity and lack of inhibition that creates an optimum opportunity for development. Children's sheer excitement, wonder and enthusiasm for the world around them makes for an era of rapid development. In the preschool years, the child's lack of concern for external constraints allows for a free exploration of both their material and conceptual world.

Primary school teachers who have introduced technology into their curriculum often comment that technology activities are a valuable vehicle for all types of learning. This can include developing generic skills such as collaborative group working or problem solving, or more specific development of math or science concepts. The technology activity often promotes a rich learning environment for a whole range of learning opportunities, thus providing an added value. Giving children a broad based experience of technology at a young age through which the foundations of technological capability can be consolidated and enhanced provides a basis from which to develop in a coherent and continuous way.

Technology appears in several guises within curriculum documentation and taken, as a whole, three different formulations are clearly identifiable: courses that focus on developing awareness of technology (e.g., exploring it's impact on society), courses that focus on developing competence in technology (e.g., learning about electronics, learning how to shape a particular material) and courses that focus on developing capability in technology. These latter courses develop a pupil's holistic capability to put ideas into action to develop the made world.

There is an important place for the development of awareness and competence (and indeed the three focuses are not necessarily mutually exclusive). But, it is the inclusive, holistic approach to developing capability that is the important focus with children in primary schools. Some might find this wrong faced. It could be argued that it is better to start with developing an awareness in young children and then building from this. But this would deny the important features highlighted by Ron Ritchie, and in particular the priority of learning through practical activity, so vital when considering the learning needs of young children.

Developing children's skills assists in the creation of positive attitudes such as self esteem and motivation and these attitudes in their turn help establish the conditions in which technological capability can thrive. However, such attitudes can be both built and destroyed through engagement in technological tasks and so it is important that children work in an environment that is at the same time supportive and challenging. They need opportunities to work on tasks that are within their capability, but that still have the potential to stretch them, where risk taking and failure are not seen as negative or handled destructively.

The teachers, who have by and large come afresh to technology activities have developed insights both by working through challenging tasks for themselves and by involving pupils in such activities. The resulting view is that the children should be involved in risk taking situations, where failure is seen as a positive learning experience and that this approach can prevent the children from placing "false ceilings on what they can learn and accomplish".

Technology is intrinsically a value laden phenomenon as developments are always driven by the needs, wants and aspirations of individuals or groups of people. Diverse needs mean that individuals will often perceive the impact of any technological solution differently - some may see a solution as good, while for others it is an unmitigating disaster. Because this value laden position is a reality, it is important that children are encouraged to see the issues surrounding any technological decision, and to be involved in the decision making in a meaningful way. For this reason, primary teachers are increasingly involving children in technological tasks where the value positions are clear to the children and are presented in a way to which they can relate, such as the ways in which choice and use of materials impacts the environment.

Developing positive attitudes towards their peers and understanding the value of working with others is an important aim of technology education. Within this, the importance of children developing respect for each other, and in particular accepting the rights of all to engage in technological activities is vital in creating a nurturing learning environment. This means that it is critical that technological activities take place in an atmosphere where stereotypes are countered and differentiation strategies are utilised to allow all children to realise their potential. This is particularly so in primary schools as value positions can be adopted at a very young age, and if not challenged by real and positive examples can become intransigent.

Technology activities are particularly rich in potential for allowing all children to succeed, thus providing living proof to challenge negative assumptions. However, in order to support the development of all children, particular consideration needs to be given to the ways in which young children learn and consequently the range of experiences that teachers need to structure for them. In order to operate effectively, children must develop a range of contributory skills - procedural, manipulative and communicative. This must occur alongside conceptual understandings, both of how to make things work and how to meet people's needs and wants. Few people would disagree with this standpoint, but the way in which such contributory skills are best developed often is the cause for disagreement.

The ways in which primary education has developed in different parts of the globe will relate very much to the traditions and ethos of the culture in which it has developed. In the United Kingdom, while there are differences between one school and the next, the overarching model of learning in primary schools is one which is seen as "child centered" and in which children are viewed as active learners. Any debate about approaches to teaching and learning technology in education must consider the often conflicting claims for priority in addressing educational or vocational needs. For very young children, the focus and priority must be on their educational development.

The issues of the development of their technological capability should not be clouded by introducing such issues as the economic well being of a nation or how a work force is going to be trained for the next generation. This is not to say that we shouldn't be concerned for the future of the children and do our best to ensure that they develop their potential to lead happy and satisfying lives as adults. It is more to suggest that the specifics of the technological experience of six year olds should not be planned by looking at the skills required for them to pass examinations at the end of compulsory schooling, or those that will allow them to become the mechanical engineers, architects or food technologists of the future.

By developing a more generic potential from a young age, this next generation may be more comfortable, confident, and secure in their own capability. As a result, they may be in a better position to utilise it flexibly across a wide range of settings. Where these skills are developed through an integrative, holistic approach, there may be greater propensity for them to be utilised in a broad range of settings, hence furthering the potential of technology education. It is also important that knowledge and skill are not seen only in terms of vocational development.

The introduction and development of knowledge and skill on "need-to-know" basis can serve to enhance the developing capability as young children resolve tasks in a satisfying rather than frustrating way. Readiness for learning is an important concept - trying to introduce a new skill or concept to a learner too early can at best be wasteful of time and at worst damaging to their confidence if they perceive themselves as a failure. The concept of teaching knowledge and skills in technology on a need-to-know basis, introducing new material to children at the point they need it to further pursue their designing and making, pays attention to the notion of readiness, but goes further to highlight the importance of teaching something new in context.

Technological capability is an integrative capability that draws on and draws together a person's knowledge, skill and understandings. Because of it's integrative nature, the capability is best developed in an holistic way, and hence assessed in a holistic way. This approach allows teachers to build an overall picture of a child's capability, within which they can look to diagnose specific strengths and weaknesses. Once identified, action for development can be taken within the context of the child's overall capability, identifying strategies (that can perhaps be shared with the child) to develop specific areas, such as a child's ability to plan, to reflect, to make and so on.

Developing technological capability requires teachers to structure activities and inputs in such a way that what children learn, in terms of procedures, concepts and skills, is "taught not caught". Moreover, the children should be active participants in this process. This is not to marginalise experiential learning or to discount the potential of serendipity, but rather to identify the importance of teachers taking an active role in determining both the what and the how of the learning. This means that teachers need to have the personal knowledge, skill and confidence to resource this, which, because of a lack of training provision, is not often possible.

Earlier the importance of the 'readiness' of children to learn was emphasised. This concept is equally important when considering how teachers can be supported to engage successfully in technology education. Very few primary teachers have received formal training in the teaching of technology education. Even those countries that have decided to introduce compulsory technology education into their primary curriculum, and who have set up training programs to facilitate this, have a back log of unprepared technology educators teaching in primary schools. The key areas to be addressed in helping teachers move forward include:

1) developing teacher's understanding of what technology education is;
2) helping them see how the work they currently do, and the experience they already have, can be adapted to allow technology activities to grow from the work already undertaken with the children;
3) developing their confidence in their ability to build on and utilise their previous experience;
4) identifying a broad but manageable range of activities for teachers to start from, and providing them with personal, hands on experience with the activities before they embark on them with children;
5) providing opportunities for teachers to share good ideas and good practice and build a repertoire of successful activities.

Challenges of Infoage Education

Information Technology can be used to simply automate the procedures currently used in organisations; but existing activities are much more likely to be at least rationalised, in order to take advantage of new possibilities that the technology creates; and in some cases they need to be substantially re-invented. The impacts on organisational processes are therefore generally noticeable, and can be quite profound. The expectation is that the changes will have considerable benefits, but these will often be felt only in the medium-term.

Commonly, the short-term impact on the organisation and its profit is negative, as investment is undertaken, once-off expenditure is written-off, and disruption occurs to the existing routine. The impacts on employees are almost inevitably significant. Many people currently in the workforce have not been well conditioned for change by their education and training, and are not mentally well-prepared for it. Quite commonly, those workplaces most in need of radical re-design are those in which the employees have been in a settled (and increasingly inefficient) mode of operation; and hence the shock of change is all the greater. People's work-patterns, and the skills required of them, may be quite different from those that have, until recently, been conventional.

Capabilities in relation to computers and communications are vital. The conventional approach of deferring particular kinds of transactions, and processing them occasionally in batches, may be replaced by on-demand handling of clients' needs. There may also be impacts on working-hours, such as customer support extended beyond the traditional 9am-5pm time-frame. The location at which the work is performed may also change, with more performed on client's sites, or at home.

These changes can result in major impacts on organisational structure as well. Increasingly, the primary focus is on business processes, and the hierarchy of managers and supervisors is being regarded as less important. Organisational units that run as mini-empires are often inefficient because they are resistant to change for extended periods. When IT is implemented, such units are likely to be dis-established. The looser workgroups which replace them, rather than being associated with other, similar groups are more likely to be linked along the business chain by which value is added to the organisation's raw materials to produce its finished products. Beyond the workplace, communities are functioning differently because of I.T. Some of the more important impacts are in the following areas:

— changes within existing communities;
— the emergence of electronic communities.

One of the tendencies of 'successful' I.T. applications is that they deliver a great deal of what each individual needs at a workstation or playstation. So there is less reason for each individual to get up and walk around. Apart from being physically unhealthy, this also reduces people's direct interactions with one another, which is the cornerstone of existing communities. Another negative impact is the reduced need for humans to work, arising from the productivity in white-collar work which I.T. is delivering. For many people, this results in lowered self-respect, and reduces their commitment to themselves, their community and their society. New forms of communities are emerging, based on USENET, Fidonet and the Internet during the last 20 years, and the explosion in popular use of the Internet during the last 3-5 years.

Electronic communities have quite different characteristics from traditional communities based on physical proximity, and on cultural, ethnic, religious and professional commonalities. Society as a whole, and individuals within society, are being significantly affected by IT. Some of the more important impacts are in the following areas:

— equity of access to information;

— pricing;

— regulation;

— consumer rights;

— privacy; and

— electronic freedoms.

Currently, the Internet and the world-wide web are accessible for relatively low costs. A related issue is that of pricing, particularly of information gathered and made available by government. The information infrastructure comprises many components, including high-bandwidth backbones, regional capacity, 'tail-ends' out to user sites, and workstations in public institutions such as schools and libraries. The cabling, network hardware and software, and communications protocols need to respect a sufficiently common set of sufficiently advanced standards and protocols that inter-operability can be achieved; and yet the whole undertaking must incorporate sufficient flexibility and adaptability that future advances can be exploited. It is also important to appreciate that the scheme is intrinsically supra-national, or global rather than just regional, national or local. Many difficulties must be confronted, however. One which has attracted attention is the question of regulation of the information infrastructure. A great deal of attention has been focussed on sexually explicit material, particularly that which would be refused classification by the Censor, and which would accordingly be illegal to possess or distribute in printed or filmed form.

Other risks exist, however, such as incitements to violence, including extreme forms of racist behaviour, and instructions on how to prepare explosives, commit crimes and perform terrorist acts. Concerns also arise about the impact of IT on consumer rights. The challenge for governments is to impose controls in support of the public interest, without destroying the free, open and self-regulatory nature of the Internet.

The 'equity of access to information' issue was discussed earlier. The other side of the same coin is the question of the privacy of personal data and personal communications. In general, activities on the Internet and the world-wide web are identified: the postings individuals read, the goods and services they enquire about or purchase can be monitored and recorded. The growth rate in traffic on the information infrastructure has been so great that its impacts on privacy have so far been more theoretical than real.

But both commercial, marketing interests, and government agencies whose functions include data surveillance, are taking an increasing interest in the information that can be gleaned about individuals from their behaviour on the Internet. Many people are arguing for considerable electronic freedoms for individuals. One example is the movement to ensure that any individual is free to use any form of cryptography. This means, on the one hand, that individuals will have the same rights in cyberspace as they do in the real world, to obscure their conversations from people who may be listening.

On the other hand, it makes the tasks of national security and law enforcement agencies in combating organised crime and terrorist groups more difficult than it otherwise would be. At a more general level, IT is affecting aspects of the national economy, in particular in the following areas:

— employment levels;

— the distribution of income; and

— access to education and training.

Productivity tools of many different kinds are enabling organisations to perform functions with fewer resources, and in many industries this means that fewer humans are being employed. The rate of new job creation by emergent industries appears not to be high enough to take up the slack. The result is that, even when the economy is improving, unemployment levels are staying high, participation rates are falling, and more people are in part-time employment than was the case in the past. Some people are fairly well-adapted to part-time pay for part-time work, especially at particular stages of their lives, such as the period when young children are at home or needing care after school, and in the years preceding full retirement from the workforce.

Unfortunately, many of the people out of work in Australia at present are recent school-leavers, many of them matriculants, and in some cases even tertiary-trained graduates. In the past, people who had never been employed, and had therefore never had an occupation, were rare exceptions; but we may be seeing the emergence of a whole class of permanently unemployed and unemployable. Many others among the currently unemployed are people who have not only an economic, but also a psychological, need to be in employment.

IT is succeeding for the organisations that use it, and may do so for the customers of those organisations. It may also do so for the people who continue to be employed. There is therefore a need for society to deal fairly with the people who don't have jobs as a result, at least in part, of IT's success. Measures of several kinds are needed:

— to ensure that the distribution of income is equitable;

— to enable the unemployed to achieve individual quality of life; and

— to address the problem of whole communities within which few members are employed.

The law establishes the framework within which people's rights and responsibilities exist, and can be enforced. IT is having an impact on some aspects of the law, including:

— evidentiary questions;

— intellectual property, especially copyright; and

— unintended contingent liabilities.

Another legal issue is that of intellectual property law in general, and copyright in digital materials in particular. Similar concerns arose with the widespread use of photocopiers, and of audio and video tape recorders. Digital technologies are much more complex, and their impacts more profound.

Copyright statements accompany many on-line databases, but it is not entirely clear how enforceable these statements are, and what steps governments need to take to protect the rights of the authors. Another matter of concern is whether organisations providing electronic services to other corporations and the general public may be incurring unintended contingent liabilities. For example, the contents of some web-pages might be interpreted by the courts as representing advice, and a person who relied on it and suffered because of that reliance, might have a case in negligence against the publisher. Alternatively, a page might breach another person's copyright, or contain material whose display is illegal in some other jurisdiction.

Some people are concerned about the cultural integrity of their regional or lingual groups. The President of France has expressed concern about the predominance of english on the Internet, despite the fact that 47 countries in the world speak french. Critics suggest that the use of english is a convenience, and not an attempt by the U.S.A. and other english-speaking countries to dominate the world and destroy local cultures. On the other hand, equity and freedom of speech and information may be considered to be basic rights within the so-called 'advanced western world', but this is not the case in all cultures, particularly those in which a particular religion plays a major role. There are also ways in which national sovereignty is threatened by the global information infrastructure. The law can be difficult enough to impose within a geographical jurisdiction; but when data storage, information communication, and funds, all flow freely across national borders, the ability to enforce the law, and to collect the taxes on which government agencies depend, may be greatly reduced. Many people are sceptical about the ability of nations to survive the challenges that the global information infrastructure represents, and anticipate breakup of large countries into smaller communities.

An important part of the national sovereignty question is the integrity of the currency. During most of the twentieth century, currency has been mainly issued by national governments. Things approaching supra-national currencies have emerged but these have been subject to considerable influence by national governments. Now new forms of currency are beginning to appear that may within a few decades completely undermine the ability of central banks to provide a framework within which all flows of funds take place, and to influence the level of activity within the national economy through the instrument of monetary policy. Stored value schemes using 'smart' chip-cards, of which several variants were launched in Australia during 1995-96, are one threat.

A much larger one is electronic cash, also referred to as E-cash, or digital cash. Electronic cash is based on cryptographic techniques, and enables organisations and individuals to make payments in a secure manner, directly over the information infrastructure. It performs several functions, including that of:

— a medium of exchange, which is immediate, convenient, cheap, and relatively difficult to trace; and

— a store of value, which is no more intangible than existing deposit balances recorded on a remote computer, but is much more readily spirited across national borders.

Electronic cash is capable of subverting traditional monetary controls. And it is technically proven, and in the course of being implemented. Rather than just listing problems, we need to work out what to do about them. The key terms that are used in this regard are:

— risk analysis;

— risk management; and

— controls and audit.

Risk management strategies encompass the following alternatives:

— Proactive Measures

— Avoidance (don't use risky forms of IT, e.g. neural networks)

— Deterrence (motivate people not to do risky things with IT, e.g. make people liable in criminal and civil law)

— Prevention (put barriers in the way of people who might do risky things with IT, e.g. ban client-side scripting products like Java, install firewalls, avoid connecting company networks to the Internet)

— Reactive Measures

— Detection (have means of knowing when people make risky uses of IT, e.g. install virus-testing software on all workstations)

— Recovery (have means of repairing the damage, e.g. data backup and recovery procedures)

— Insurance (share the risks around, e.g. compulsory computer centre fire and earthquake insurance policies, duplicated processors, uninterruptable power supplies)

— Non-Reactive Measures

— Tolerance

In Australia, Information technology students played a significant role in ethics education and shaping their perceptions and deliberation of situations involving ethical considerations. The effects of cumulative ethics education with regard to students' ethical behaviour when dealing with various computer oriented situations.

Students' perceptions of the amount of training they received in computer ethics differ from one student to the next, regardless of their level of education.

The burgeoning information technology sector has placed greater on the ability of its professionals to deal with a range of situations which have ethical implications. Educators must take responsibility for providing effective training that identifies and stresses the importance of appropriate ethical behavior especially as it relates to the use of computers. The information technology revolution are now facing affects all aspects of our daily life. The issues that arise from such rapid changes include the impact on our social values as well code of ethics. While the motives of unethical behaviour are not new, the manifestations in the IT (information technology) context present a challenge to our society. As more and more people are now employed in the IT industry and society depends more and more on IT, it is important that IT professionals graduating from Universities have the right ethical attitude and understand the conflicts they are facing when tempted to carry out unethical behaviour. The Cognitive Dissonance theory is based on a few assumptions. The central assumption is that human beings cannot tolerate cognitive inconsistency.

The theory states that dissonance (psychological inconsistency) exists whenever one cognitive element conflicts with another cognitive element. The magnitude of dissonance is a function of the importance of each cognitive element and the number of dissonant and cognitive elements that exist at that time. Once dissonance is aroused, there will be a need to reduce dissonance. Dissonance may be reduced in many ways, including revoking the decision that causes the dissonance, lowering the importance of the decision and adding consonant elements.

Thus, from the Cognitive Dissonance Theory perspective, when a person who believes he/she is a good person is tempted to commit or has committed an act of unethical behaviour, cognitive disssonance arises. The belief that one is a nice and honest person and the thought that one is about to commit or has committed an act of unethical behaviour (such as copying software illegally) causes conflict, dissonance or psychological discomfort. After the theory is introduced, the students are given scenarios of unethical behaviour and requested to analyse the unethical behaviour from the perspective of the theory.

In United States, the fair use doctrine has been called "the most significant and perhaps murky of the limitations on the copyright owner's exclusive rights. This limitation becomes even more murky when applied to the educational use of copyrighted material on the global Internet, either in the form of downloaded material or material that has been "uploaded" for use by others. United States university deans revealed that the deans had a very limited understanding of what the act entailed and the relationship between the law and the guidelines. As a result, American educators tend to err on the side of conservatism, while other countries interpret simple accessability as unlimited license.

The global nature of the Internet has further complicated the issue of fair use of Internet material. Cultural differences and social cohesion are examined as key variables in examining the international implications of copyright. One of the biggest challenges to intellectual property right protection is derived from the global access of the Internet and the varying, culturally based, perceptions of individual or community rights regarding knowledge products. The copyright enforcement policies of countries should be expected to vary and this idea is explored using the values topology created by Hofstede. Specific examples of differences between countries are reviewed to provide insight into how the cultures perceive the protection of intellectual property. Educators using the Internet to provide class materials need a clearer understanding of the implications and boundaries of "fair use". As the computer, the Internet, and multimedia become more involved in education, teachers need to be aware of the implications and limitations of fair use from both a legal and ethical perspective.

The new communication and computer technologies has generated a host of ethical problems, and some of the more pressing concern the moral notion of privacy. Some of these problems arise from new possibilities of data collections, and software for computer monitoring. For example, computers can now combine and integrate data bases provided by polling and other means to enable highly personalised detailed voter profiles.

Another cluster of problems revolves around the threat to privacy posed by the new possibilities of monitoring and surveillance. For example, telephone tapping, interception of electronic mail messages, minute cameras and virtually undetectable listening and recording devices give unprecedented access to private conversations and other private communications and interactions. Possibly the greatest threat to privacy is posed by the possibility of combining these new technologies, and specifically combining the use of monitoring and surveillance devices with certain computer software and computer networks, including the Internet. Provision of an adequate philosophical account of the notion of privacy is a necessary precursor to setting the proper limits of intrusion by the various new technologies. Such an account of privacy would assist in defining the limits to be placed on unacceptably intrusive applications of new technologies. Moreover it would do so in such a way as to be sensitive to the forms of public space created by these technologies, and not unreasonably impede those new possibilities of communication and information acquisition which are in fact desirable.

As always it is important to balance the rights of individuals against the needs of the community. On the one hand there is a fundamental moral obligation to respect the individual's right to privacy, on the other hand there are the legitimate requirements of, for example, employers to monitor the performances of their employees, and law enforcement agencies to monitor the communications and financial transactions of organised crime.

2

Technology-rich Classroom

The World Wide Web and other Internet-based collaborative tools have significantly enhanced the ability to train and educate electronically. Whether the materials are a stand-alone tutorial or a full-fledged on-line workshop, the Web provides significant new functionality in transmitting information to the student and providing forums for exchange. When integrated with tools such as listservs, Usenet newsgroups, annotation facilities, and video teleconferencing, the Web can greatly increase students' level of involvement in the training experience. The Web provides an effective mechanism for integrating many of these tools into a single interface and is an ideal tool for information which is itself rapidly changing. The Web is revolutionizing some areas of discussion through increased opportunities for learning and alternative formats for information.

Hence, use of an on-line information system and electronic tutorials has been central to education and training activities from the beginning of the center. It is clear that the internet, with its ability to connect people and information around the world, is already having a significant impact on education at all levels. The lofty goal of an interconnected global schoolhouse across remote corners of the world is getting closer. Virtual classrooms are being created today for educating scientists, engineers and mathematicians, both researchers and faculty, and will provide needed experience and basic knowledge for use with other student populations in the near future.

Electronic Education System

Hardware and software vendors sometimes supply user documentation in electronic format, it is often 'command' oriented, but users often require 'task' oriented materials (e.g., the user needs to learn how to run a batch job, without prior knowledge of the names of the five commands involved) and each vendor uses a different interface for access to on-line materials. Even now that computing vendors are creating World Wide Web servers, they are slow to include user documentation, but instead concentrate on marketing information. For all of these reasons have made use of an electronic user documentation system since the founding of the center in 1985. The Theory Center on-line information system contains educational materials in a variety of formats. There are 140 items specifically designed to be instructional tools that are referenced thousands of times each month. This electronic education system not only serves the CTC researchers, but also the international research audience, and provides materials that other educators can incorporate into their courses. The types of educational materials in the on-line information system.

Electronic tutorials have been available for more than nine years. Tutorials are intended to be short, self-contained instructions on a specific topic (e.g., use of an optimization subroutine library). Each tutorial contains a short description, step-by-step instructions in using the utility, and an example code that can be executed. Researchers can read the tutorial and try the example, possibly taking the example code to use as a template for their own problem. These tutorials are task-oriented, not command-oriented.

Lab exercises have been provided in electronic format for the past two years. These exercises are intended to supplement lectures given at a workshop. The solutions to lab exercises are provided in a separate file to encourage the student to solve the problem instead of following the cookbook instructions found in a tutorial. Placing the lab exercises on-line has allowed workshop participants to more easily continue to work on the problems after returning home. Also, the on-line versions will be kept up-to-date where hardcopy lab exercises quickly become out-of-date.

During the fall of 1994 began to maintain a complete set of lecture notes on-line. Formatted as a traditional 'overhead foils', lecture notes are frequently a list of bullets which provide a guideline for the lecturer to use in presenting the materials. Lecture notes may not contain full details of the topic, but usually contain many references to other electronic materials for more information. In addition to providing continuous access to these materials for workshop attendees and other trainers, have been experimenting with using NCSA Mosaic and Netscape as the mechanism for presenting the lecture.

The students can follow the lecture on a terminal in front of them or can see the instructor's monitor displayed with a large screen projection system. Future improvements to system will be carried out to incorporate images, animation, and user-interaction forms into documents. The more advanced functionality provided by the Web and emerging search technologies to better integrate training materials, hardware and software documentation, on algorithm design and related research. Changes in these areas will continue the evolution to an increasingly effective on-line information system.

Distance education, in the form of a course offered across the Internet, is a logical next step for the Theory Center. This course is distinct from user-initiated, independent accesses to on-line materials because it will have an instructor and a registered group of participants. This brings together a community of learners into a virtual classroom where they can interact with each other. Goal is to create a virtual classroom, using methods that will fully engage the students in the learning process through an interactive, dynamic environment involving the student, on-line materials and an instructor.

There are many topics that need to be explored before being able to offer complete workshops over the Internet. These range from technical considerations to sociological aspects of learning without the existence of a physical classroom. Much results has already been done in distance education. While distance education can provide efficient utilization of scarce resources, more fair distribution of knowledge, and timely dissemination of new knowledge, limitations in its effective use exist.

On-line instructors may need to take more time for the electronic course. Limits to the number of students may be required to maintain quality interaction. While generalizations in the effectiveness of distance education are dangerous, a common set of advantages and disadvantages are emerging. The Web solves some problems of traditional distance education and brings new issues to the forefront. A leading effort in exploring this emerging world is the Global Network Academy. The Theory Center will face a number of similar issues, but will also have some unique situations related to field of instruction and the network-sophistication of intended audience. Some of the issues addressed for pilot course follow.

With traditional workshops, attendance is limited by the physical size of training facility (about 50 students). Normally this means that attendees are users and potential users of facilities— researchers whose backgrounds, computing experiences, and expectations are somewhat similar. With an electronic course, the size of the class will be limited by other non-physical factors such as staffing requirements for account administration, limited consulting support, and CPU resources required for the class laboratory exercises. An electronic course will need to have some of these same attributes in order to ensure that students find the experience worthwhile so that they complete the course. There needs to be some sense of an "instructor" for the students to interact with and the ability for the entire class to participate in questions and answers.

Designing WWW Documents

Print-based instructional materials have served well in

the past in support of student-centred independent learning. In recent times, the move to computer-based learning environments has been taken to improve the perceived interactivity of the materials. There are unique advantages among print and computer-based materials and the WWW appears to provide a means to make the most of the opportunities afforded by each. Some critical considerations in designing electronic instructional and informational materials include organisation, orientation, navigation, presentation and interactivity.

A problem facing the WWW designer is choice of the strategy that should be employed to organise the material. While hypermedia describes a particular type of learning environment, there are several forms of exposition that assume this title. The different forms of hypermedia can be described through a continuum describing the nature of the linking involved. At one end of the continuum, the links are minimal and simply act to connect nodes in a specified sequence. This form of hypermedia closely resembles conventional text and is referred to as linear. In its use, the learner is encouraged and in most cases compelled to follow an instructional sequence planned by the instructor. In hypermedia environments, there is potential to create materials with varying degrees of linearity. Further along the continuum, the links tend to form a hierarchical structure, giving learners more freedom in the choice of path through the materials. At the extreme, hypermedia can provide a totally unstructured learning environment with multiple links between associated nodes. In this environment, learners are free to move between associated nodes through referential links and very little structure is imposed and in evidence.

The choice of information organisation for WWW materials depends on the nature of the intended learning outcomes. A useful guide for selecting the form of hypermedia most suited to the nature of intended learning outcomes by suggesting instructional strategies against knowledge acquisition aims. When the instructional forms of the different forms of hypermedia are matched against the continuum describing instructional strategies, it is evident that when the materials seek to develop students' initial knowledge, for example, facts, procedures and rules of discourse, linear linking is an appropriate hypermedia form. For this type of learning, it is appropriate to create materials with a strong structure that present information in a planned and considered fashion. In using these materials, learners are required to follow an instructional sequence set by the teacher.

For higher levels of knowledge, for example, developing an understanding of concepts and principles, the less structured hierarchical and referential linking are more appropriate. In such instances, students are guided by such factors as their prior knowledge and readiness to assimilate new material. When building on an existing knowledge base, learners can benefit from the freedom to browse and explore, to inquire and seek responses to their own questions rather than following a pre-determined path of instruction. One of the major problems with the use of hypermedia as an instructional form when compared to print materials, is the orientation of the learner within the learning environment. Orientation describes the means by which users are able to identify their current position in the system, how they achieved that position and how to return to a previous position. Disorientation is a problem which is frequently observed in studies of hypermedia users and a problem which significantly limits instructional outcomes. Electronic learning materials can easily conceal much of the information they contain and it is important in the design process to provide the learner with a means to orient and move freely within the information space.

The structures provide access to the information nodes within a system together with an overall structure for the learner that is reinforced as nodes are selected and viewed. The use of frames and targetable windows provide a means for materials to continually display these structures as content is selected and accessed. A number of tutorial guides on the WWW provide good exanmples of this feature. Semantic Nets Learning can be enhanced when connections and associations between related information are recognised and made specific. The use of image maps as tools by which information nodes can be accessed and selected provide a linking structure and reinforce associations and connections between the contained information as well supporting learner orientation. The CNN Newsroom uses a concept map as alternative means to seek links.

Collaboration

A majority of contemporary computer-based learning reflect the belief that the interactions will, and should be, made by a single user. However research studies have shown that there are clear educational advantages to be derived from collaborative activities among students. The implications of this for WWW materials are that interactions and activities that engage higher-order thinking and critical reflection need to be included and opportunities presented to enable group and team work. The communications component of the WWW provides unique opportunities to enable forms of communicative and collaborative activities among networked learners. Computer-based learning programs frequently subdivide skills into small sections which are then taught systematically in a logical order. This often results in the processes requiring little thought as the students can deduce the answers correctly from the preceding parts without a real understanding of the subject. Students know information must be relevant because it is in the same part. There is no need for reflection.

More effective environments require students to reflect upon a much broader base of knowledge to solve their problem. The simple fact of being adjacent to a particular topic would be no guarantee that the information is relevant to the problem. In order to solve the problem or complete the task, the student would be required to reflect upon the whole resource by predicting, hypothesising, and experimenting to produce a solution. The increased use of hierarchical and referential links and associations in documents reduces the linearity of the instructional pathway. Activities that encourage reflection and metacognition through increased levels of learner control can assist students to focus more attention onto their own thought processes. Most computer-based learning programs are designed to be used quietly with the learner selecting, pointing and clicking in silence. Being able to speak the vocabulary and tell the stories of a culture of practice is fundamental to learning and yet the use of many WWW documents allows the knowledge to remain tacit.

More effective learning environments ensure that the resources are used within a social context with students working in groups, discussing the issues, back, presenting findings, interviewing and debating the issues to ensure that students have the opportunity to articulate, negotiate and defend their knowledge. The use of e-mail and other communicative activities supported by the WWW provide opportunities for articulation enabling tacit knowledge to be made explicit. The third constitutive element of an effective WWW learning environment is the role of the teacher and the procedures by which the learning materials are implemented. Learning environments in interactive multimedia suggests the following strategies as powerful adjuncts to enhancing teaching and learning with the WWW:

Coaching describes the action of the teacher in providing guidance and help in a learning setting while scaffolding represents the support provided in the form of skills, strategies and links that the students are unable to provide to complete the task. Enhanced achievement is obtained when the strong support is provided initially (the scaffolding) and then gradually removed as the student becomes able to stand alone. Many designers of WWW instructional materials attempt to create documents that are self-contained resources that include everything the student needs to learn a particular topic. However, there are many individual learner characteristics that cannot be accommodated in a single WWW document. There have been some attempts to create intelligent systems for the WWW, adaptive hypermedia, but currently this role is still best performed by the teacher.

The teacher's role in coaching, observing students, offering hints and reminders, providing feedback, scaffolding and fading, modeling, and so on, are powerful enhancements to any learning situation. The implication for the instructional design of WWW materials is that the teacher's coaching role needs to be acknowledged and addressed, with suggestions and strategies planned and taken for implementation with students. Much of this planning is independent of the actual development of the WWW materials. Measures and assessments of achievement and outcomes from instructional settings play an important part in the teaching and learning process. Frequently with computer-based learning, assessment measures bear little semblance to the environment in which the learning has taken place. Assessment can no longer be viewed as an add-on to an instructional design or simply as separate stages in a linear process of pre-test, instruction, posttest; rather assessment must become an integrated, ongoing, and seamless part of the learning environment'.

The enhanced interactive capabilities of the WWW provides the means for assessment of student learning to extend beyond conventional essays and examinations. More reliable assessments can take the form of evaluation measures such as portfolios, summary statistics of learners' paths through instructional materials, diagnosis, and reflection and self-assessment. Much of this can be achieved and supported through appropriate design of WWW documents and learning materials. There are many factors which influence the learning that will be achieved from the use of computer-based learning materials such as CD-ROM based multimedia and materials designed for the WWW. Currently most attention in the design of WWW learning materials, and multimedia, seems to be in the planning and development of the materials themselves. While this is an important activity, it must be accompanied by consideration of two other factors in the learning process, the learners themselves and how the materials will be implemented.

In the development stages of WWW instructional materials, try to consider not only the content to be delivered but also appropriate learner activities and support and implementation strategies. Building on the experience gained through many years of CD-ROM based multimedia development. The future most multimedia used in higher education will be delivered through networks and platforms such as the WWW and that research and development in this area is very important.

Types of Interaction

Many education and training institutions are looking at using the Internet for distance learning with renewed interest since the advent of graphical interfaces. Browsers, like Mosaic and Netscape, and the Web are making possible, the application of on-line multimedia technology in the distance learning environment. Distance educators are interested in this technology because of the potential improvements for interaction. The types of interaction, it is suggested that interaction typically found in traditional CAIs may fulfill only part of the interaction needed in effective distance learning programs that use on-line tutorials. Design recommendations are offered for HTML-based CAIs that may help incorporate a total interactive support package for distance learners.

Students in distance education are learners who have chosen this mode of result usually because of the flexibility it offers; students are not bound by time and location. This is evident considering that most distance learners are not isolated geographically from an institute of higher learning and could have chosen a program in traditional education instead. But interaction is often sacrificed for this gain in flexibility as a consequence of the barrier of distance between student, peers, and instructor. This interaction has individual and social dimensions where individual interaction is interaction between the individual and the learning material and social interaction is interaction between two or more people concerning the learning material. Both forms of interaction are necessary for learning and should be ensured through the technology of the media and the design of the distance learning presentation.

Within the Courseware Development Team, a committee of the research group, members are looking at multimedia uses in traditional education for applicability to the computer media communications (CMC) distance learning environment (DLE). An initial review of how on-line tutorials were implemented at NSU revealed that most uses followed a hierarchical menu level approach with some interaction between student and tutorial and very little interaction between student and teacher despite the potentiality of the hypertext environment through the Hypertext Transfer Protocol (HTTP) and associated HTML. Consequently, the team is investigating on-line CAI designs to improve individual and social interaction. Traditional CAI learner control strategies are being looked at for improving individual interaction and Common Gateway Interface (CGI) programme support for social interaction.

Learner control is a characteristic of CAI where students are allowed to make decisions on the content and context of the CAI presentation, as opposed to program control where the learner has no opportunity for this type of interaction. This is not to say that programme control CAI does not allow individual interaction. It is well understood that an individual can mentally interact with the knowledge domain of such programs, just like one interacts with a good novel, but cognitive learning theories suggest an interaction with the environment that shapes schemata and learner control is used to help facilitate this type of interaction. The interaction implementation strategies in traditional CAI have primarily included content strategies where interaction is achieved through learner control techniques such as content control, sequence control, pace control, display (strategy) control, and feedback control. Context strategies are also used to give the learner control over the background setting and text density. Content control allows the learner to control the selection of the content he or she wishes to learn.

The CAI has a set of topics from which the student can select. Sequence control, like content control, allows the selection of subjects, but in this case, all the subjects or topics have learning objectives related to the overall course goal and the learners' control is over the sequence of the topics to be learned. Pace control is typically considered one of the strongest advantages of CAI. It is a form of individualized instruction which allows the learner to take as much time as necessary to learn the lesson concepts. Usually, this type of control involves some kind of student tracking system so users can take up where they left off from the last CAI session. It also includes features that allow the student to control movement from one screen to another.

Display control allows the learner to choose one of several displays which cover the same subject matter or concept. A rule, and simulation, all covering the same material, can be provided to allow the learner to select which options they personally need in order to grasp the lesson concepts. Feedback control allows the learner to either defer to computer controlled feedback or select options on the feedback mechanism. Context control includes learner control over the background of the material and text density. Principles and concepts can be presented in different environments which serve as the backdrop to the lessons and also provide a form of situated learning. Mathematical concepts, can be presented as business, or scientific problems and the user is free to choose the situation. Text density refers to the density of the material presented—bullet statements as opposed to explanatory paragraphs, etc.

Learner Control Classification

The learner control classifications by examining the strategy of the controlling implementation as opposed to the control mechanisms. They found that whatever type of control mechanism used, the implementation strategy generally fell into two categories.

— An approach where the entire lesson is presented to the student and the student has positive control to eliminate unwanted material.

— An approach where only basic and fundamental principles are presented to the student and the student has positive control to add to the material. They called these two approaches as "FullMinus" and 'LeanPlus' respectively.

Learner control can be applied through a Web structure although some content methods may be more difficult than others. The HTTP protocol allows branching of documents and can be used for both content control and sequence control. Pace control is already inherent in distance education and providing a student tracking system within the CAI would require additional programming or CGI support. Feedback control is limited by the basic HTML standard but can be improved greatly with the addition of CGIs. Display control and context methods of control appear well within the educator's ability to implement using HTML. Learner control strategies like FullMinus and LeanPlus also seem possible. Another challenge using HTML in CAI design actually results from the strength of the Web. The Web was originally designed to facilitate the growth of non-linear knowledge bases throughout the Internet. Users are free to enter works at different locations (documents) and they can establish these entries within their own home pages.

Students' power to enter the works at any location may not meet the CAI designer's intent so the design of each document within the work must be able to stand alone so that confusion is not caused by references to previous topics not visibly seen. This capability to enter the work at any document location, on the other hand, might be a method of learner control unique to the distance learning environment, yet to be explored. When one examines past studies on learner control in CAI in traditional settings, a general impression is formed that interaction, discussed in these studies between a student and CAI, is a representation of interaction (social) between the student and teacher/designer who authored the CAI programme. It probably goes without disagreement, this implied social interaction may actually occur by other means; communications with peers or SME.

The central problem in the distance learning environment is that the effectiveness of the programmed interaction through learner control strategies may not be sufficient, in itself, to improve social interaction in the absence of other communications. There has been unanimous agreement among distance education theorists that two-way communications is an essential element in distance education. By looking at the learning situation, it helps to visualize where social interaction strategies are needed to improve student-teacher interaction in HTML-based CAIs.

Social Interaction

The need for student-to-SME knowledge base interaction. In this scenario, the student is taking the CAI and is confronted with an issue of special interest the student wishes to explore further by browsing related literature immediately. If the instructor has been maintaining a home page with an index into the knowledge domain, HTML links could be strategically placed into the tutorial to allow the student to deviate from the planned course of instruction to investigate related material. This is a unique form of learner control that can be implemented on the Web which goes beyond traditional CAI uses of branching. With Web tools, totally unplanned and unprogrammed excursions are made available to the student. The student is literally interacting with the instructor's knowledge and the instructor's Internet links to the knowledge base of the subject matter. Now consider the need for student-to-SME direct communications. In this scenario, the student is taking the CAI and is confronted with material that is confusing, or the student wants to add information, or take issue with the presentation.

The student wishes to communicate with the instructor on the subject. In traditional CAI, the student can normally have face-to-face human interaction with the CAI subject expert at the next scheduled class session but in distance education, this is not always possible. The distance learner must make a mental note and then contacts the instructor by telephone, e-mail, or written correspondence and this delay may cause the spirit of the message to be diluted. With HTML/CGI forms technology, it would be possible to add hypernotes write capability to the on-line CAI that would allow email communications with the instructor while taking the CAI. Finally, consider the need for instructor-to-student communications. Just as any teacher wishes to monitor student progression in the class room in order to help redirect when necessary, in this scenario, the instructor wishes to monitor the progress of students as they interact with the CAI.

The following considerations are offered: It is possible to have no learner control by establishing the work (presentation) as a single document (file). The entire work would look much like an electronic version of a printed paper and would have no links to any other documents. Very basic learner control could be added to the document with a table of contents that links to internal document anchors. The advantage of this traditional approach to on-line Web documentation are the file can be easily printed or downloaded by students and less links may offer less access time; an economical concern. Improving interaction will lessen these advantages and should be cautiously considered in light of different learning styles but used where appropriate.

Once the work is divided into linked documents, learner control over content and sequence greatly improves, but will be unrestricted in that the user can establish their own home pages and links to augmented sources. The author should exploit this capability in the learner control strategy instead of considering it a liability, and should realize that the work may evolve into a complex web of information (improving social interaction in the cyber community) by the learner's actions as additional links are established to other sources. Such a learning environment may likely be reserved for advanced learning situations. Since a FullMinus learner control strategy is apparently more effective than a LeanPlus strategy in traditional uses of tutorials, an on-line tutorial that introduces new concepts should contain as much required information as possible and students can use the learner control capabilities of item two to filter unwanted information.

On the other hand, a LeanPlus strategy might prove more useful than the FullMinus strategy in a tutorial that is designed to reinforce concepts previously learned. The tutorial could list other Web source documents or search engines that the student could linked to if desired. Text density is another area of great promise for on-line tutorials. Tutorial authors can develop two or more versions of each document within the work that would allow the learner the choice between abbreviated or expository information. Despite the unrestricted content and sequence control inherent in an HTML work, authors should establish navigation features within each document that help users to move within the design originally envisioned by the author.

The user, of course, is free not to use the navigation features, but for beginners, these features might be an indispensable help aid. An orientation strategy should be used to add visibility to the structure of the entire work. Graphical presentations have been shown to be more effective at this than text based. A map of the presentation should be included and navigation methods to the map should be available within each document. The graphical map, however, must use HTML alternative methods since some students may only have text based browsers or have elected to turn off the graphical capabilities of advanced browsers in order to improve performance in data transfer. The protocol for HTML forms allows data input by the user into a database file or electronic mail. Link objects could be added to the tutorial that students could activate when they need to contact the instructor.

The instructor could review comments daily and respond to students as necessary. Using HTML supported by CGI, implement tracking methods to gauge student performance through CAIs. Design them so that student problems can be easily identified and instructors can give feedback to students as early as possible. The use of learner control strategies in traditional CAI has been result extensively and is still on-going as technologies change the learning environment. Additional research in learner control for on-line applications, however, will be needed to understand individual interaction in the on-line environment, with all its own technological challenges and constraints. Also needed are studies in the design of on-line CAI to see if there is any impact on social dimension of interaction.

The increased use of educational technology is only a minor aspect of the redesign of courses for flexible delivery, but the technology can be a source of considerable stress both for staff and for students. As more teachers make use of the Web for delivery of courses and for interaction with students, the careful choice of software tools can reduce this stress by providing interfaces that are easy to drive, thus reducing the cognitive overhead for staff and for students. The still-developing WEST educational management system provides a simple consistent interface to many of the communication and interaction tasks teachers need to carry out in constructing and managing courses that make use of the Web.

Over the next few years many of us will benefit from and also be burdened by the need for learning to extend beyond the physical location of the University and also beyond the early years of life. The most predictable outcome of this change is that teaching will increasingly make use of the Internet, the vast and continually growing web of networked computers that can be accessed by students both from their homes and from the University. Many new skills to maintain competency as educators. Most University staff enjoy learning, but the methods of learning they mastered may not be as comfortably available to students in joint future. Society moves from universal secondary education to universal tertiary education will increasingly be subject to pressures designed to influence us to make the University experience more accessible, allowing busy people to fit it in to their working day when they see fit.

Students' lives by reducing the need for them to travel to the central University site in order to engage with the University experience.

Flexible Teaching

Introducing flexible teaching involves a lot more than merely converting lecture notes into Web pages. On the visual level the differing characteristics of the media require quite different formatting of textual material. On the organisational level, breaking the lock-step of classroom sessions and mass concurrent teaching will require much greater flexibility on the part of the bureaucracy, as exemplified in the negative by the current insistence of many institutions on students' personal attendance for re-enrolment. Considerable anguish may be caused for lecturers who will need to rewrite much of their teaching material if they are to avoid high dropout rates and take advantage of the increased opportunities for their students to experience the realia of a subject. The loss of face-to-face behavioural, gestural and tonal cues may give rise to many misunderstandings and will require particular attention in educational designs.

Many teachers have to imitate existing familiar teaching situations and strategies when delivering instruction via new technologies, and the problems this approach causes in the successful adoption of the new technologies. Besides raising the need for staff development in the use of new teaching media, they point out that two of the 'missing' components in conventional distance education are student/instructor interaction and class collaboration. Retaining the immediacy of these learning interactions will not be accidental. New communication technologies now allow us provide much more of these than in conventional distance education, but the design task is not trivial even for single-user interactive media. Learning from a well-made Open Learning package may be like having a good human coach or tutor, but the skills involved in preparing that package are quite different from those required to deliver a useful lecture. Beyond these issues, however, many operational difficulties arise in use of such educational communication technologies, as experienced in the adoption of earlier technologies in face-to-face teaching. The use of video-projection from a computer to replace the use of static overheads does not dispose of the need to prepare a certain amount of static overhead material as a backstop in case the video-projection system fails. For differing reasons, this doubled preparation will be repeated as introduce more flexible methods into teaching.

Both the face-to-face or audio-taped lecture and the Web page need to be prepared if provide increased flexibility rather than merely a substitution of delivery media. While in an ideal University there would be sufficient support staff to relieve the lecturer of the technological aspects of this task, experience suggests that the present dearth of such support staff will continue, a lack both in absolute numbers and specifically of those who are sensitive to and have some allegiance to the needs of teaching as opposed to the needs of machines. Teaching staff will have to bear at least part of the preparation burden, just as many now prepare their own teaching aids such as overheads. The temptation for many will be the direct conversion of existing material for electronic presentation. This will create a market for conversion software, able to ease the task for relatively non-technical teaching staff, as programs such as Powerpoint have done over the last few years. In the short term many electronic lectures will be created, driven by the pressures of time and lack of support and justified as being at least partial steps along the way to providing more flexible learning conditions.

Situated Learning

Learning activities that lack social interaction usually fail to evoke emotional involvement from learners and thus deny the learners engagement with the culture of the 'community of practice'. Most classroom learning activities involve knowledge which is abstract and out of context, is unsituated. Problem-based learning approaches tend to reduce these effects and well-made multimedia interactives can restore some context to the learning, but teaching that interposes current communication technology between the learner and the teacher risks engaging the student with the wrong 'community of practice'. The technologically-aware lecturer needs to be sensitive to the danger of having students apprenticed to technology rather than their chosen discipline.

In contrast to the pressure towards 'remote-control' teaching will be desire to maintain the personal contacts that as necessary and valuable in understanding and guiding students. Mass teaching has reduced this contact and the use of educational technology can sometimes lead to further depersonalisation. Teachers seek to ameliorate this depersonalisation by, trying to make the mass lecture a two-way communication: standing at the front of the theatre while showing slides: setting aside times when they are available for personal discussions in their office. The increased use of technology dictated by move to greater flexibility needs to be leavened where possible by increased interactions between student, teacher and learning community. The techniques and technologies which isolate learners from one another, seeking rather to identify tools which, because of their ease of use, are more likely to used both by students and staff.

Integration

Over time easier methods of achieving these varieties of educational interactions will be developed. The GUI Web browser integrates image and context, enhancing understanding and usability beyond the Gopher browser that gave access to similar material. Just as a Web browser allows file transfer, gopher access and email with little cognitive overhead required of the 'reader', so the interface to the varieties of communication required in delivering a course and managing student interactions must be simplified. It will ease this exchange by reducing the need for the student to master the use of a variety of programs. These new integrated tools will also make it easier for teaching staff to manage the flow of material to and from their students. By making the process easier, the new tools leave more mental energy available for creativity and communication. Consequently both creation and communication are more likely to occur. A variety of such learning management tools are being introduced as many Universities around the world reinvent their particular wheel.

Where learning material is essentially static and designed to be read and copied by students, it can be stored on a university's Web server computer and maintained by emailing updates to Computing Centre staff directly or by file transfer using tools such as Fetch. If, however, you want to retain the more personal elements of teaching that many staff find rewarding, you may be interested in communicating on an individual level with your off-campus students, receiving and managing student responses, assignments and enquiries online, promoting class-wide discussion of a topic or even adjusting course material for individual student differences. WEST is a system developed at University College Dublin which makes it easier to manage the creation and delivery of learning materials over the Web. The ease with which this system can be set up and maintained puts it well within the technical ability of the majority of university computer users.

Once the server is running, all lecturer tasks can in fact be carried out from any computer on the network. If the current interest in using the Web to increase the flexibility of course offerings is maintained, personal Web servers backed by management systems like WEST could proliferate on lecturers' desktops, just as presentation software has become a standard part of the lecturer's toolk it. Just as HTML and its associated tools offer 'multimedia for the rest of us', desktop educational support tools may add real value to the 'ubiquitous servers' in educational institutions. The system presents a simple consistent interface making heavy use of buttons and forms, as shown in the Figures below, thus avoiding the need for staff and students to master a variety of different interfaces to achieve the mix of messaging most appropriate to flexible learning. The WEST system provides facilities for individual registration and controlled access by students who are part of a class studying some course; it allows the allocation of learning materials as Web pages to students or to the whole class; it provides one-to-one messaging between student and tutor and between students. It also allows one-to-many messaging similar to a bulletin board or news group. Students can send messages to their tutor and submit assignments. They can also send messages to specific students or to the entire class through the open-to-everyone discussion list, where they can read what other students have written about a course discussion topic. The simple interface of the discussion list is easy to understand and use but lacks the thread feature of Internet News.

Tutors can receive messages and assignments from students, reply, mark and return assignments or have them automatically marked and returned. They can make announcements to the whole class or address individual students. Any of the variety of messages can include HTML code and thus include hypertext references to other resources on the Internet. The use by students of simple Web server software will allow multimedia messaging between all participants. Administration of the system, including the addition, alteration or removal of content, classes and students. HTML must be written or pasted into the form as shown below. This is a far cry from the ease of such Web-page authoring tools as Adobe PageMill, but the body section of pages created in a Web editor can be copied and pasted into WEST.

WEST does not keep track of student accesses, nor of how far a student has progressed. These are important features for staff administering courses for remote students, whose flagging motivation may require restorative action unnecessary for on-campus students. Many teachers will need to learn new ways of teaching as flexible teaching and learning become an expected part of course design and delivery. The design of material for learning at a distance is not a trivial task, but it will be made easier if the hurdles of Educational Technology can be lowered. Hopefully tools such as WEST will be improved without losing their ease of use and will allow teachers to incorporate a variety of message streams into their course material, to build in interactions that involve their students. If teachers can manage learning processes on the Internet without becoming amateur programmers, they will be able to give more attention to encouraging student-teacher and student-student interactions that are appropriate to the new media and the new learning environment.

Learning Communities

Learning is an attribute not just of individuals, but of different organismic entities in society at levels ranging from local to global. More than ever has it become a key determinant for the survival of the world, rather than merely a condition for survival and well-being of the individual in the world. An ever growing variety of technologies offers powerful opportunities to support and develop it. However, the perspective on learning as it transpires from current practice and discourse reflects little of the multiple ways learning can be looked upon in the context of what is known about such issues as lifespan development; complex adaptive systems, cognitive science, mind/brain research; or multiple intelligences. Considerations that people have different learning styles and notions about how learning connects to local culture and knowledge systems are equally often absent from such discourse and practice.

Looking at what the world has achieved in terms of education, one sees an impressive institutional infrastructure linked to a firmly established network of interests. Berenfeld refers in this regard to the monopoly of education. Teachers constitute the "largest single group of trained professionals in the world" Within the existing structure, they are not only a major facilitating factor, whose importance, incidentally, is less and less reflected in the social and material recognition they receive, they are also a leading force against change. "Education is increasingly necessary and less and less possible, due to its cost." Against this background, it is to the credit of distance education that it has been increasingly successful in positioning itself as a valid alternative. To establish its validity, however, distance education had to model itself on the same ideological underpinnings that also condition mainstream educational provision and show that it was equally or more effective or at least nearly as good.

Thus it should be no big surprise that the probably best known definition of distance education as "an educational process in which a significant proportion of the teaching is conducted by someone removed in space and time from the learner" is based on the same assumption that underlies the mainstream educational process, i.e. that a main condition for learning is that there is someone who teaches. Moore and Kearsley advance the following more elaborate definition of distance education: "

> Distance education is planned learning that normally occurs in a different place from teaching and as a result requires special techniques of course design, special instructional techniques, special methods of communication by electronic and other technology, as well as special organizational and administrative arrangements."

While this definition clearly puts the emphasis on learning and while it does not explicitly refer to a person who teaches, it is no less based on the notion that teaching is a necessary condition for learning to take place. For this very reason, the two authors express a clear preference for the term 'distance education' over that of 'distance learning'. Such a position is unnecessarily restrictive as it is based on the notion that the best distance education can do, is to approximate as closely as possible the learning-through-delivery-of-teaching model inherent in the face-to-face mode. Centuries of educational development have not succeeded to avoid that close to a billion people in the world are illiterate, that more than 130 million school-age children do not go to school and that many of those who do, often end up with learning achievements that fail to sustain or that are irrelevant to their needs. There is thus a clear indication that yesterday's educational solutions are inadequate for today's problems and there can hardly be a stronger signal that doing more of the same is not a valid solution. It is equally apparent that today's solutions are an inadequate option in response to the challenges of the future.

The main conception underlying education continues to be that learning is something one does once in a lifetime and that it is essentially undertaken in preparation for the rest of one's life. It is thus best done during the early stages of one's life. For those who, for whatever reason, missed the boat, there are second chance opportunities, often via the distance education mode. Whatever is done in addition to this boils down to learning every now and then in the course of one's life in response to specific needs to maintain or upgrade professional skills or to adapt to new demands of the work environment. There is no strong notion of lifelong and lifewide learning as an essential ingredient of life itself, as something which is more than, a simple means to acquire a particular skill or to become familiar with a specific area of knowledge. To respond to the dual challenge to on the one hand overcome the failures of the past and on the other to be responsive to the demands of the future, the world needs to move beyond fixed modality delivery options based on the teaching-learning dichotomy. It needs to put learning and the learners at the center of its concerns. It needs to break through the barrier of looking at learning as the consequence of something that is being done to people instead of something that is done by and with people.

The relationship between learning and empowerment is a dialectic one. Learning leads to empowerment, but it will do so only if the learning process itself is premised on the notion of the empowered learner. The learning-through- delivery-of-teaching model, whether face-to-face or at a distance, is contrary to that notion. Until a couple of decades ago, learning in preparation for the rest of one's life was still generally a valid option. School systems provided the main mechanisms to put that option into practice. A ministry of education could claim it had things under control if an adequate school system existed and people pertaining to the various socio-economic strata of the population felt they had access to that school system according to their aspirations and needs. People could be reasonably sure that, after completing their education, they were well prepared for the rest of their life. The time to learn was over, and real life could begin. This, however, is no longer the case. In today's world, and that of tomorrow, the notion of learning to earn a living, and even that of learning for life, is no longer a valid one. Learning is no longer for life, but learning is life and life is learning. Learning is pervasive.

Individuals and societal entities—organisations, local communities, cities, whole nations even—are in constant need to adapt to change. While they do so, they generate change themselves. Learning is not only an essential requirement to allow people and groups of people to adapt to change, it is at the same time the most effective mechanism to ensure that change is being generated in a way that takes into account the ecological dimensions of its impact on others. Change occurs at a pace which has brought an essential dimension of unpredictability in the lives of people. It has become impossible to foresee one's life and thus to plan one's education accordingly, as if it were part of a linear sequence of events. Adaptation to change can no longer be managed as a generational process—it has become intra-generational. Most of the existing educational establishment is out of tune with this reality.

The notion of learning as an essential condition of growth of complex adaptive systems is currently perhaps best exemplified by the learning organizations. Survival, gaining and retaining competitiveness, are obviously much more immediately felt urgencies in the business environment than in the traditional closed school environment and its supporting institutions. It is there that one sees complex adaptive systems in action at a scale that may generate interesting models for the reconceptualization of learning environments in general and the diffusion of organizational learning beyond profit making institutions. This should lead us to think of learning communities—rather than just learning individuals—as crucial elements in the conception of facilitating environments for learning.

Most schools, and for that matter also the traditional distance education institutions, are not learning communities. They are simply closed organized structures designed to turn uneducated individuals into educated ones. They do themselves, as social entities, not learn and are not designed to do so. Quite to the contrary, if one considers their tremendous capacity to often totally ignore and resist change, the conclusion would seem to be justified that they have been designed not to learn. Learning communities in the sense referred to above are essentially open systems. They interact and are in dynamic equilibrium with their environment, i.e. with other learning communities. They are not fixed. Individuals may be part of different learning communities depending on context and circumstance. The term 'distance education' is now often associated with that of 'open learning'.

'Open and distance learning' is thus frequently used as a single concept, suggesting that distance learning is by necessity an open process and that open learning is mainly accomplished in the distance education mode. The use of terms such as 'open university' and 'open school' adds to the confusion. The dimension of openness of such institutions is often limited. In addition, both 'open learning' and 'distance education' are frequently presented in contrast to and as separate from so-called conventional or traditional education. Distance education has as such little to do with the notion of openness as it appears in the concept 'open learning community'. Systems that use it as a modality can be equally traditional as and no more open than many conventional systems, based on the face-to-face mode. Yet, distance education has much to contribute. Thanks to the development of distance education have important experience of self-directed and self-motivated learning and increasingly also of multi-channel approaches, which often include distance learning modalities. By nature, open learning communities cannot be established by an outside agent. They are constructed by those who pertain to them. They are themselves the result of a constructivist learning process, involving a variety of partners whose roles can best no longer be dichotomized as either those of learner or teacher.

The process of their construction is helped along by the existence of a facilitating open learning environment which contains the essential ingredients and building blocks that learning communities will want to make use of. It is such environments that must build. In building up propitious environments that are conducive to the generation of open learning one faces a dilemma. There is important existing infrastructure and practice that one would like to build on. However, part of that same infrastructure and practice reflects much of what is in urgent need to be changed whereas another important part of it has hardly received recognition as belonging to the learning environment. It is perhaps in the first place necessary to consider the broadness, complexity and unpredictability of learning.

Constrains of the Internet for Education

The history of Education cannot be told apart from its technology. From orality to literacy, from manuscripts to the printed page, from text to hypertext, the prevailing technologies supporting education have defined its very nature. Stopping short of technological determinism, acknowledge the chicken-and-egg relationship between technology, education, and society. The possibilities which education brings to society depend upon the affordances of the undergirding technology. The term affordance to describe a potential for action, the perceived capacity of an object to enable the assertive will of the actor.

There are many objects in environment. Some ignore, some adapt to, and some appropriate for assertive will. It is the objects in this last category which fall under the the definition of affordances. Certain objects afford opportunities for action. An affordance is a value-rich ecological object that is understood by direct perception. Perception informs the individual of affordances. Action transforms affordances into effectivities which extend human capabilities. The eyes afford perception, the ears listening, the hands manipulation, the tongue and vocal cords afford utterances. Natural affordances emerge into effectivities through use in conscious activity. The hand of an infant, though attached, is a separate object. The infant is amused by it, studies it, tastes it, touches other things with it. Soon the infant learns to use the hand to manipulate other objects. In the process, the hand gradually transforms its object-ness to subject-ness.

The child becomes less conscious of the hand as she uses it as an extension of her own intentioned will. The affordance becomes an effectivity. Technology and media are affordances to the extent that they promise extended human capabilities of seeing, hearing, and uttering. Tools are affordances to the extent they offer extended human capabilities for manipulating things in the environment. Through use, skill is acquired and the object becomes an extension of ourselves. These artifacts are transformed from affordances to effectivities. Five thousand years ago the affordances of orality and rhetoric were extended by the technology of written text. Writing enabled the precision of recorded memory. It afforded cognitive communication across time and distance.

The written word introduced constraints of grammar and syntax, but out of these constraints emerged stability and permanence of language. It was a means of representing and archiving human knowledge for later retrieval by one's self or by another. In the period approaching the late middle ages, the power of literacy began to spread to the merchant class. Manuscripts were extremely costly, reproduction of a single copy required weeks of labor by an established member of the literati. Often, students copied their own texts, transcribing oral recitations by a lecturer/reader. Learning to read and write was the privilege of an elite few. For those without means, a literate education was characterized by extreme effort supported only by primitive techniques and rudimentary tools. Entry into the literate community was not possible without great personal sacrifice. Manuscripts, the objects that enabled this intention, were affordances for acquiring literacy. The rise of the universities in Europe and the neo-classicism associated with the return of the Crusaders in the thirteenth century drove unprecedented demands on manuscript production. In a previous era, this renaissance would die before it began, lacking the infrastructure to support the propagation of knowledge. But modern technology was on the horizon. The mid fifteenth century saw the convergence of several unrelated developments: the wine press, oil-based ink, block printing, and finally, movable type.

The power of print technology was in the hands of an emerging ruling class. The printing press was an affordance for Martin Luther to assert his Ninety-five Theses, challenging established authority. The emerging years brought the Reformation, the Enlightenment and democracy. The bourgeois state triumphed over monarchies. Liberalism instituted basic rights and freedoms: The rights of private property, freedom of self-expression, and freedom of the press. These 'self-evident' rights spread throughout the Western world. They were the expressed freedoms for all citizens, but they were particular effectivities for those who owned property, those who possessed the skills associated with self expression, and those who owned or controlled the presses. The modern age became an age of reading and writing (mostly reading). Book learning changed the nature of basic education throughout the West.

Education in the twentieth century retains a content-centered paradigm of institutional affordance. However, this has been a century of major curricular reforms. The changes have reflected a more diverse and complex society with a broader range of values and priorities. As society continues to diversify, as the need for technical skill increases, as the world changes faster than textbooks and lesson plans can keep pace, the emphasis on curriculum content is giving way to a focus on the learning process. Constructivism, considered radicalism a decade ago, is the dominant perspective at most educational conferences. Content objectives are giving way to a focus on skills development, instructional designs are giving way to learning environments where students define the central tasks, including how the learning should be monitored, assessed and adjusted to achieve the desired outcomes. Such strategies bring flexibility to the educational process, adjusting to continued change in a postmodern world.

Today's information technology enables the transition from modern to postmodern, no less than the printing press enabled the transition from pre-modern. Technology has changed the way consider content. In a 14th century university classroom, a manuscript of Rhetoric was likely the exclusive source of information. That was a constraint imposed by the technology. Today, download Rhetoric in seconds, but can also download related texts, commentaries, research studies, historical perspectives, ad infinitum. Scan these texts with the eye of a computer, discovering patterns, linking them to allied texts, offering multiple dimensions of textual analysis.

In recent years, a prime objective in media development has been the quality of interactivity. This has been especially true with educational media, starting in the 1950s with Skinner's 'teaching machine', evolving in the 70s to 'response-and-branch' CBT, progressing into the '80s with Apple's 'poke-and-see' hypercard and ultimately, 'answer-vision', the hopes behind interactive video. All of these are examples of closed systems in which the content is pre-defined, responses are anticipated, and action is controlled by the designer alone. Interactive video pioneer, Andy Lippmann, lamented the inherent weakness of such closed systems. None seemed to satisfy his definition of interactivity, the mutual, autonomous, and simultaneous activity of both participants working toward a common goal.

Lippman's criteria are fundamentally unreachable under the constraints of a closed technology. But the open architecture of the Internet transfers interactivity from an affordance of designer control to that of user control. From flat textual domains to full motion video, the Internet transforms the mechanistic character of modern media into a postmodern phenomenon, shifting agency from author to user. The designer has lost control, but the medium has gained credibility. The real world is waiting on the other side of the terminal. In reality, learning is distributed between the medium, the learner and the context. There is nothing inherent in the Internet that guarantees learning. But in a specific context involving learning activities, such as research, collaboration, self expression, and reflection, the Internet offers multiple affordances, so numerous that it may be a mistake for us to treat it as a medium. It is really an infrastructure which brings together media, tools, people, places and information, expanding the range of human capabilities. If treat the Internet as an infrastructure, then can draw comparisons between the Internet and other infrastructures which society has come to rely upon for learning and education. The Internet offers multiple affordances, not unlike other infrastructures for learning. And suggest that the Internet overcomes significant factors which have historically constrained the others. A comparative analysis may illustrate our point.

The publishing infrastructure has been the primary conduit for knowledge in the modern world. It requires capital and considerable labor to disseminate information in published form. Between the modern author and the reader is an infrastructure which includes editors, type setters, printers, binders, and a complex marketing and distribution organization. For a publisher to print anything today, a business case must guarantee proper return on the investment. At a time when society's need for diverse information expands geometrically, the number of corporations which control the publishing infrastructure continues to decline. While freedom of the press is extended to all, its affordance is an exclusive privilege.

The concept of free expression is changing as pass from the modern to the postmodern. Having the right to free expression is something entirely different than having the affordance of expression. Just as technology challenged exclusive control of knowledge in the fifteenth century, exclusive control of information is challenged again today, this time by the Internet. On the Internet, there is no central control: no editorial board to determine acceptability, no screening committee to determine relevance, no financial board to assess marketability. Each author is her own publisher. Each reader, his own editor. All that is required for publication on the World Wide Web is a personal computer, a modem, and a user account on an Internet server. Students and faculty enjoy such affordance at most major universities. Commercial providers offer public access at at costs comparable to telephone rates. Public schools are on the World Wide Web, publishing hypertext productions by teachers and students.

Imagine the possibility of students providing a web page that is a genuine service to the Internet community, something the students care about, and something that is needed. Consider a likely niche, such as a weekly review of children's television, a computer help system for low-tech parents, a FAQ database on snow boarding, roller blading, etc.. Writing for an audience of peers around the world is likely to elicit motivations that go beyond teacher expectations. To the extent that students use the opportunity to present themselves before a world wide audience their writing will be influenced by motivations of ethos, style, and delivery: the elements of classical rhetoric. The constraining factors are likely to include the teacher's comfort level with the technology, and her willingness to yield control of the resource to her students, the level of her perception about the Internet as an affordance for learning goals (not necessarily for other institutional goals).

The affordance of world wide public expression is something new for all of us. With the Internet, the perceived capability of self expression in a world-wide forum can be extended realistically to the common person. However, there is no expectation that each person will embrace it. Consider Socrates' reaction to literacy. Consider the skepticism of most Americans, saturated with the hype of technology and media. By definition, an affordance is the the potential for action. This implies that there is a will toward specific action. Implied in the affordance is the intentional desire for action and the recognition that the object can enable one's intentions. For the reader, a fundamental constraint has to do with the accuracy, veracity and reliability of online information. This is not to say that accurate information can't be found on the net.

The implication has more to do with the shifting role of the reader in assessing the accuracy, validity and applicability of materials which were heretofore left to editors, experts and peer professionals. An additional skill will be essential to basic education—the skill of abductive logic. The goal in abductive logic is not ultimate truth. It is the ability to advance one's inquiry. Abductive logic is the logic of signs: the ability to extract meaning from a given set of circumstances and then to adjust one's inquiry as new information unfolds. The skill of Sherlock Holmes is critical skill of the information age. There are Internet tools to assist in this process. They are called robots or agents. An agent is a software tool that is dispatched to accomplish a specific task. As information continues to abound on the Internet, will need such tools to assist us in searches.

The standard tools are search engines which accept a set of keywords from a user and return a list of resources in rank order, listing first those which best match the search criteria. The problem is that searching on a single word can yield overwhelming and debilitating results. Stone suggests that the ideal model for an agent is the graduate student. Graduate students are trained to do research. They can assess the usefulness of new information within in the context of the present inquiry. A research assistant is attuned to a professor's work, and is able to gather the kind of information that fits a given research programme.

Instead of submitting a simple keyword, phrase or boolean expression, the user can submit a complex object: a bibliography, a list, an index, an article. The intelligent agent discards incidental and common words from the text object, prioritizes the remaining words by the frequency of use. Multiple searches ensue, and results are evaluated against the model object. Tools of this nature produce quality results for minimal time investment, overcoming the debilitating constraints of too much information associated with simple searches. The fundamental characteristic of the Internet is that it cannot be controlled. While local legislation can influence pockets of control, the Internet is a world wide phenomenon, with no one in charge. In more modern times educators could easily control what their students read and direct how those tender minds might be shaped. The educator's role was largely in the selection of good and proper literature, selecting resources which combined intellectual development with moral edification.

The learner's moral edification was directed externally by a teacher, by an editorial committee, or by a school board. Today the classics of literature, fine essays and poetry still abound. They are rapidly finding their way online. The supreme difficulty in the Information Age will be the ability to restrict a learner's education to a 'sanctioned' body of literature. The discipline required of learners in the postmodern age goes beyond that of all previous generations. The role of education in the age of information will be the development of disciplined readers, skilled in the art of abductive logic.

In contemplating what the future might hold for education it is sometimes useful to gaze into the past. Knowledge in the modern period followed logocentric patterns with one-to-many relationships. The postmodern period promises yet greater dissemination marked by a many-to-many relationships. The developments brought about by technology allow for new possibilities. Agency is shifting from center to periphery, from teacher to learner, from author to reader, from librarian to researcher, from curriculum to context. The affordances of public expression have exploded, allowing any school child to represent herself before a world-wide community of learners.

The affordances of information retrieval have advanced to the point where a simple query can yield a flood of information. This is where the modern and postmodern minds collide. To the modern mind, there is too much information. The world is exploding with ideas and perspectives that cannot possibly be consumed. But to the postmodern mind, attempts to control information are futile and naive. What control exists in the postmodern world will emerge—not from the center, but from the periphery. The genie is out of the bottle. There is no chance of forcing him back.

Modern educators have learned how to utilize constraints of the environment as a means of scaffolding in the instructional process. Constraints can limit a field of information, making it more manageable for learners. Constraints of grammar and syntax are necessary for language acquisition. General social behavior is learned from constraints involving etiquette and protocol. But the freedoms that suddenly emerge are frightening. The modern educator might be tempted to impose artificial constraints on the medium in order to control and manage the educational environment. Software is available at this moment which allows a teacher or parent to filter information and restrict access to objectionable sources on the net. Such artificially imposed constraints may be necessary in the short run to mitigate controversial dilemmas and situations that challenge traditional thinking. But are persuaded that the real challenge for education is to discover the natural constraints associated with a highly connected and deeply fragmented world.

A set of rules or policy guidebook for the postmodern will not be found. But out of distributed knowledge, are seeing the emergence of a new ethic with an entailing structure of distributed control. The challenge for the postmodern educator is to discover the capabilities and natural constraints associated with distributed pedagogy for scaffolding learners in the age of information.

3

Learning without Boundaries

The ease of use or 'transparency' of technologies such as the World Wide Web and video-conferencing makes it much easier than in the past for faculty to develop technology-based learning materials and course delivery. The World Wide Web for instance allows a teacher easily to adapt materials created for lecture or classroom use and present them as attractive colour graphics and text. Once the materials are created as Web pages, it is a simple matter to make them available for off-campus as well as on-campus students. In an increasingly competitive environment, and where technology-based teaching is increasingly open to public inspection, the organisations that will survive, as with any of the other new knowledge-based industries, will be those that provide services that the public values, at a better price and quality than the competition. For the extra cost of using technology to be justified, it needs to be accompanied by the reorganisation of the teaching process, moving away from fixed, scheduled group instruction to more flexible and individualised modes of learning. There are several components of quality in technology-based educational materials. New technologies then are likely to remain marginal, despite high levels of capital investment, and will merely add costs to the system, if do not at the same time deal with structural changes in institutions, and in particular if do not make fundamental changes to the ways organise teaching.

Vision for Teaching

'Visioning' is indeed a technique that allows those working in an organisation to understand the full range of possibilities for teaching and learning that technology can facilitate, and the possible outcomes, acceptable or otherwise, that might result from its implementation. It helps people working in an organisation to identify and share certain goals. In particular, an institution needs to define what balance it wants between face-to-face and technology-based teaching. An institution could for very good reasons decide not to go down the technology-based teaching route and place special emphasis on face-to-face and personalised teaching. It is likely though to be a very elite and high cost institution. Alternatively, an institution might wish to vary within its structure the degree of dependency on technology-based teaching, giving more emphasis for instance to face-to-face teaching at the graduate level, and more to technology-based teaching at the undergraduate level. Lastly, other institutions may make a clear decision to emphasise technology-based learning throughout all its teaching. Another issue that should be covered in a vision statement is the extent to which an organisation sees itself operating on a local, regional, national, or international basis, and the implications of that for courses offered and student services.

This is important because technology-based teaching does not respect political or geographical boundaries. For instance, regional colleges may need to redefine their role if students are capable of accessing the college's standard courses from other, perhaps more prestigious institutions, anywhere in the world. The vision included several detailed scenarios of teaching and learning for different types of learners. There were several key features in the vision:

— a mix of teaching models, from programs delivered entirely in a face-to-face mode to courses available entirely at a distance; it was envisaged though that most students would take a mix of face-to-face and technology-based teaching over the life of a full degree program;

— an increase in the provision of technology-based non-credit, certificate and diploma programs, aimed particularly at mature students;

— learning materials developed as discrete modules for multiple uses, i.e. the same CD-ROM might be used for on-campus and distance undergraduate students, as part of a certificate program, as continuing professional education for individuals, and as a stand-alone CD-ROM for employers/companies;

— more flexible admission and access, particularly for mature students, through the use of technology-based learning, allowing more students to be admitted to the university.

One of the main challenges of making technology-based teaching a core function is to extend its implementation from a relatively small number of enthusiasts and early adopters to the main body of the teaching force. This means introducing a strategy for inclusion, to ensure that all faculty are encouraged and supported in their use of technology for teaching. Because initially the funding for innovation was held back from general operating grant, the university applied the same principle as the government: faculties' operating budgets were reduced proportionally, then they were encouraged to put forward ideas as to how to spend 'their' proportion of the operating grant held back by the university for applications of technology. Many universities have old buildings without adequate conduits for wiring, or asbestos fillings within walls that need to be removed before modern cabling can be installed.

Many faculty and staff will not have a computer or know how to use one. Servers will need to be installed within each department, and networked to other servers on campus. Internet connections with the outside world will need to be established, and ports and other communications facilities installed to enable students in residences or off-campus to access the main university campus, or satellite campuses and other institutions to be linked. While such a technology infrastructure strategy is absolutely essential, unfortunately it is often the first—and sometimes the only—strategy adopted by universities: build it and they will come. However the technology infrastructure plan should be driven by, not lead, the university's overall vision and strategy for its teaching. There are in fact three levels of support required to fully exploit technology. The most obvious is the technical support, the people who make the networks operate and service the computers and telecommunications. At the second level are media production and services, those who produce educational products or supply educational technology services, such as interface designers, graphics designers, video-conferencing managers, or graduate students who do HTML mark-up. At the third level are those that provide educational services, such as instructional design, faculty development, and evaluation.

The major part of physical infrastructure, such as networks and major equipment purchases, is usually funded from capital budgets, and as such is less likely to compete for funds that impact directly on teaching, such as general operating budget. The cost of the human support though does compete directly with funds for teaching and research. Furthermore the human cost of infrastructure support is recurrent, i.e. has to be found each year, whereas physical infrastructure is often seen as a once-only investment, although rapid advances in technology and hence the need continually to replace or update networks and equipment make this a dangerous assumption. As a consequence, the human support side is often underfunded. Probably the most consistent complaint across universities from those responsible for technology applications is the inadequacy of resources for technical support. Even so, the further down the chain, from technological support to educational support, the more difficult it becomes to secure adequate resources. If the network crashes, its impact is obvious; the value of an instructional designer is much harder to sell when funds are tight.

Many of those that do have computers have machines that are not suitable for multimedia or internet access. There is also a chicken and egg issue here. If students are not required to have a computer for their studies, they are less likely to purchase one. If students who are thinking of purchasing a computer are not given clear specifications as to what is needed, they are more likely to purchase a less powerful model. There are several strategies that can be used to provide support for student access to computers. One is to provide computer labs on campus for students. Once again this is a useful start-up strategy, but in the long run it becomes unsustainable as the primary source of student support. There are several drawbacks to relying on computer labs for access. The first is that as the need to use computers for learning increases, either capital investment costs get out of control, or students' lining up for access reaches unacceptable levels. Secondly, given the rate of technological change, computers in labs quickly get out of date.

More importantly, it requires students to access learning from a specific place, often at a specific time, if they have to book, thus removing one of the main advantages of using technology, its flexibility. There will always be a need for specialist computer labs, for those subject areas requiring exceptionally high end or specialised machines and software. There will also always be a need for on-campus access through plug—in ports or drop-in labs for casual use. However, in the long run the most flexible and most cost-effective approach is to encourage students to provide their own computers and internet access. Such a policy though cannot be implemented unless it is clear that students will need a computer, and that means ensuring that there are sufficient courses designed to exploit fully the instructional benefits of using a computer.

Lastly, while technology may open up access to some and deny it to others, computer ownership is not the main obstacle to university access at the University of

British Columbia. Many more potential students are denied access by restrictive grade point average entrance requirements, arbitrary prerequisites, residency or attendance requirements, and barriers to credit transfer from other institutions. If a primary purpose of introducing technology-based learning is to increase access, these admission policy issues need to be addressed as well.

The newer technologies are quite flexible in that they can be used in a variety of different ways for teaching. Technologies can be used to replicate traditional forms of teaching; at the same time, they can be used in quite new and different ways, depending on the imagination, skills and resources available to the teacher or learner. Nevertheless, despite this variability, certain trends in the use of technology are evident. It appears that some technologies lend themselves more easily to certain approaches to teaching and learning, while other technologies lend themselves to others. There is no super technology that can meet all teaching and learning requirements, so technologies need to be mixed and matched to the educational purpose. Thus we find that instructional television and video-conferencing and certain applications of the World Wide Web tend to be used primarily for information transmission in a didactic style, very close to the classroom lecture model.

Although CD-ROM technology is often used merely to replicate a book (i.e. a didactic style), but with better graphics, animation, audio and video, a number of applications that more fully exploit the technology are emerging. Thus CD-ROMs are increasingly being used to simulate human interaction (for language teaching), for representing expert systems, such as forestry management, and for problem-solving approaches based on scientific methodology, through for example the use of virtual laboratories. These approaches to learning enable students to apply their learning to para-realistic situations, to test their own ideas and use their own experience, and as a result to make and test decisions drawing on their previous learning, or even learning facts and principles during the process of decision-making.

The Web is a particularly interesting technology in the way that it is evolving. It has the ability to combine all these various approaches to learning. For instance, WebCT, designed at the University of British Columbia by Murray Goldberg, is a Web authoring system that combines didactive and collaborative learning tools, as well as a student learning management system, allowing subject experts without any specialist computer skills to construct their own courses. The limitation of the Web at the moment is bandwidth and the power of desktop machines, which make it difficult or impossible to run the more powerful applications needed for expert systems, complex simulations and problem solving. However this will change quite rapidly. These technologies enable more powerful applications of such teaching methods in more flexible and accessible forms for students, with also the potential for economies of scale. Furthermore, what all these technologies have in common is that, when well designed, they enable learners, irrespective of the subject matter, to develop skills of information navigation, acquisition, and analysis, application of knowledge to new situations, new knowledge creation, and decision-making, all skills essential for survival in an information society. In terms of change strategies, these new approaches need to be tested and developed not just in a narrow setting of a particular class or course, but in a system of teaching as a whole, where appropriate replacing, not adding to, conventional teaching methods. Thus technology-based teaching needs to be built into the mainstream teaching, and not offered as peripheral or optional learning for students.

Teaching with technology is not something that can easily be picked up along the way, as something to be done off the side of the desk while engaged in more important or time-consuming activities such as research. The most common form of training given to faculty is to show them how to use the technology. This though is starting at the wrong place. Many faculty need to understand *why* it is important to use technology for teaching in the first place. It has to be related to the changing environment in which universities find themselves, and in particular to the changing needs of learners. Some basic understanding of the teaching and learning process, and in particular the different kinds of teaching approaches, and the goals they are meant to achieve, need to be understood.

The faculty need to understand the different roles that technology can play in teaching, and how this alters the way that teaching needs to be organised. Only then does it make much sense to train faculty in how to use a particular piece of technology. While this sequence may be logical, it is unlikely to be the most effective way to help faculty develop skills in using technology; 'show and tell' and hands-on experience are most likely to lead to this full range of understanding. Nevertheless all four aspects need to be deliberately targeted in faculty development. University teaching is probably the last craft- or guild-based profession. However, the changing nature and variety of learners, the growing complexity and volume of knowledge, and the impact of technology on teaching now really require that university teachers should have formal training and qualifications in instructional methods. This should eventually become a condition for tenure. Even more fundamental than faculty training is the need to change the reward system for faculty. While many universities have statements that equate teaching with research for tenure and promotion, the reality in most research universities is quite different: the only criterion that really matters is research. Thus there is no point in pouring millions of dollars into infrastructure and computers and multimedia unless the faculty reward system is changed.

Teaching ability must become in practice at least equal to research for promotion and tenure. The good news though is that technology-based teaching is usually more public, more observable, and hence more easily evaluated than conventional classroom methods. Furthermore, multimedia technologies provide an excellent means to convert research knowledge directly into teaching and into promotional material for the research itself. Another way to reward faculty is to ensure that revenues generated by the use of technology by a department flow back into that department, and do not get swallowed by the central bureaucracy. Innovative mechanisms need to be developed for faculty (and other creative staff) to share in rights and royalties from the development of generic educational software and learning materials. Lastly the very sensitive issue of faculty agreements needs to be addressed. There are short-term advantages in leaving things loose, but technological innovation will become unsustainable as faculty become more experienced, suffer from increased workloads, and find that they are still unrewarded.

Technology Use Classrooms

Modern technologies have transformed many aspects of life, including how we communicate, how we spend free time, and especially how we work. As life and workplace demands have changed as a result of this "technological revolution," so have conceptions of the skills and knowledge children will need to become successful adults and the relevant educational experiences they should encounter while attending school. As a result, technology, specifically in the form of computers and the internet, has become a major focus of education policy and reform in recent years. National, state, and local initiatives have provided schools with computer hardware and software, allowed schools and classrooms to connect to the internet, and supported technology-focused professional opportunities for teachers. As the numbers of computers and access to the internet in schools have grown, so have the number of questions being asked about the extent to which these technologies are being used in schools and classrooms and for what purposes.

Over the past 20 years, education technology has been a major focus of reform and policy at the federal level, as well as at state and local levels. Such initiatives have been guided by the goals of increasing the availability of computers in classrooms and schools, assisting schools with internet access, and providing resources and guidance for teacher training and the integration of technology into the curriculum. The availability of computers and the internet has increased significantly in the nation's schools and classrooms. This increase has been coupled with initiatives aimed toward understanding how best to use technology to improve teaching and learning and training educators to use technology effectively.Existing research on education technology includes a small number of national studies that describe teachers' use of technology, as well as their training to use these tools. Specifically, this research suggests that most current and past uses of education technology have typically supported traditional notions of teaching and learning.

In the early 1990s, the practice of using computers for programming had declined considerably and an emphasis on using computers as a tool for learning content had emerged. However, the primary use of computers remained drill and practice in elementary schools in the early 1990s. In high schools, it was classes on computer education, and middle schools provided a combination of drill and practice and computer education. Finally, as the decade of the 1990s progressed, school computer use had shifted to some degree to reflect a greater emphasis on problem solving and in-depth learning and less emphasis on drill and practice and basic skills. Approximately 10 percent had used computers to solve problems in natural science. Using a nationally representative sample of teachers, the Teaching, Learning, and Computing found that CD-ROM reference and surfing the internet were more likely to be assigned as classroom activities than games and traditional drill-and-practice applications. However, many of these newer uses have been limited to a small proportion of teachers and students.

Teachers are in fact using computers or the internet generally more frequently to complete a number of instruction-related tasks than to augment instruction itself. For example, they may use these technologies to help prepare for classroom instruction (e.g., to access research on best practices, download information to present in class) or to complete administrative tasks (e.g., to record and calculate grades). In the area of technology, teachers may have learned about how to use computers and adapt their teaching from a variety of sources—teacher preparation programs (for prospective teachers), professional development activities (for practising teachers), and informal learning opportunities such as assistance from classmates, colleagues, or students. Professional development research suggests that teachers' opportunities to learn about education technology during traditional professional development activities are often lacking. Often described as an important vehicle for school reform, professional development activities in general have been widely criticised for being relatively ineffective.

Specifically, they have been described as short term, devoid of continuity due to inadequate follow-up and the lack of ongoing feedback from experts, isolated from the participants' classroom and school contexts, and characterised by too few opportunities to learn by doing and reflecting with colleagues. In fact, while a majority of teachers participate in such activities, a small percentage of teachers report feeling very well prepared to integrate technology into instruction. Teacher preparation programmes have received similar criticisms. Traditional programmes for prospective teachers have been described as fragmented, superficial, and unconnected to real classroom experiences. With respect to education technology, some observers have claimed that prospective teachers are not getting the training they need to successfully integrate technology into classroom instruction. Additionally, about half of the technology training that prospective teachers get in the classroom is delivered as part of other classes (i.e., methods and curriculum classes), and the other half is provided in the form of stand-alone technology classes.

Furthermore, most teacher-preparation programs provided by schools, colleges, and departments of education do not have written, funded, regularly updated technology plans.Informal learning opportunities, in addition to these formal learning opportunities, may also provide teachers with assistance using technology. Peer collaboration, in particular, has been heralded by many teachers, researchers, and policymakers as essential for teachers' continuous learning. Teachers may benefit when they learn about technology from one another and provide one another with motivation to continue working with this resource. In recent years, policymakers have recognised that teachers and administrators need resources and organisational capacity to implement instructional reforms. On a most basic level, teachers may be more likely to integrate computers and the internet into classroom instruction if they have access to adequate equipment and connections. As the number of computers in schools has grown, so has the availability of the internet in schools and classrooms. Between 1994 and 1998, internet availability among public schools increased from 35 to 95 percent. However, availability is not the same as use.

Although the presence of computers and the internet has grown sharply in recent years, much of the technology equipment currently in schools and classrooms is from an earlier generation of technology—computers with less processing power, less storage capability, and limited capacity for being linked together electronically. Using data from 1998, Anderson and Ronnkvist have concluded that although computing capacity for instruction has improved substantially over the past several years, there are a number of "major deficiencies". The nation's schools have been increasingly challenged by policy initiatives "to do better, and to do differently", pushing teachers to change the way they teach.

At the same time, teachers face many other challenges, including rapidly increasing technological changes and a greater diversity in the classroom. With regard to technology, there is often little time in teachers' schedules to become familiar with hardware and software or to learn to integrate the new technology into their lesson plans. Lack of time to become acquainted with technology and learn to use it has been identified as the greatest obstacle to the effective use of education technology. A full-time computer coordinator, for example, may assist teachers with using computer software and hardware or adapting their teaching practice to include computer or internet use. However, less than 5 percent of all schools have such a staff member. Furthermore, where they are present, computer coordinators typically spend a significant amount of time teaching students, and much less time assisting teachers. Principal leadership has been described as one of the most important factors affecting the effective use of technology in classrooms. Principals who exhibit leadership are instrumental in modelling the use of technology in classrooms. They understand how it can support best practices in instruction and assessment and provide teachers with guidance for its use. Principals may also participate actively in professional development activities related to education technology and provide teachers with opportunities to learn how to use these resources. For some teachers, lack of principal leadership may prove to be a barrier to their effective use of technology.

Public school teachers also used computers or the internet at school for administrative record keeping, accessing research and best practices for teaching, preparing multimedia presentations for class, and accessing model lesson plans. In addition to using computers or the internet at school for preparatory and administrative tasks, the 82 percent of teachers with computers available at home also used these technologies at home for such purposes. School teachers used computers or the internet at home to create instructional materials, to gather information, as well as for administrative record keeping, accessing research and best practices for teaching, preparing multimedia presentations for class, and accessing model lesson plans. Teachers' use of technology for preparatory and administrative purposes varied by a number of school and teacher characteristics. For example, among teachers with computers available in their schools, secondary teachers were more likely than elementary teachers to use computers or the internet at school for administrative record keeping, and they were also more likely to do this at home than elementary teachers. Moreover, teachers in schools with the fewest students enrolled were more likely than teachers in schools with the highest enrolments to use these technologies at school to gather information for planning lessons.

On the other hand, teachers in schools enrolling more students were generally more likely to use computers or the internet at school for administrative record keeping and at home for this task. In addition to instructional level and enrolment size, there were a number of differences by school minority enrolment. in the percent of teachers reporting that they used computers or the internet for preparatory and administrative tasks. For example, teachers in schools with lower minority enrolments were more likely than teachers in schools with the highest minority enrolments to gather information for lesson plans using these technologies at school.

Teachers in schools with fewer minority students were also generally more likely than those in schools with the highest minority enrolments to use computers or the internet at school for administrative record keeping and creating instructional materials. Finally, teachers in schools with the lowest minority enrolments were more likely than those with the highest minority enrolments to use computers or the internet at school for preparing multimedia presentations. As is the case with teacher reports from schools with varying minority enrolments, teacher reports of whether they used computers or the internet for various preparatory and administrative tasks varied by poverty concentration of the school, as measured by the proportion of students eligible for free or reduced-price lunch.

Teachers with varying years of teaching experience differed with respect to whether they used computers or the internet to conduct a number of preparatory and administrative tasks. For example, teachers with the fewest years of teaching experience were more likely than teachers with the most experience to use these technologies at home to gather information for planning lessons and to create instructional materials. Teachers with 4 to 9 years of experience were more likely to use computers or the internet at school to access research and best practices examples than those with 20 or more years of experience. Finally, teachers with less than 10 years of teaching experience were generally more likely to use these technologies at school to access model lesson plans than those with 10 to 19 years of experience and at home to conduct this task

Public school teachers with computers available in their schools used computers or the internet to communicate with colleagues most frequently, compared to communication with parents, posting homework or assignments, and communication with students. Teachers' use of technology for communicative purposes varied by a number of school and teacher characteristics. For example, elementary teachers were more likely than secondary teachers to use computers or the internet at home to communicate with parents. On the other hand, secondary teachers were more likely than elementary teachers to use these technologies at school to communicate with students. Furthermore, teachers in schools with medium-sized enrolments were more likely than teachers in schools with small enrolments to report that they used computers or the internet at home to communicate with colleagues. Teachers in schools with large enrolments were also more likely to use these technologies at school to post homework or assignments. Teachers' use of computers or the internet for communicative purposes also varied by minority enrolment of the school. Teachers in schools with lower minority enrolments were generally more likely than teachers in the highest minority schools to use these technologies at school to communicate with colleagues. Similarly, teachers in schools with lower minority enrolments were also more likely to use computers or the internet at school to communicate with parents than teachers in schools with the highest minority enrolments.

On the other hand, teachers in schools with high minority enrolments were more likely than teachers in schools with minority enrolments of 6 to 20 percent to use these technologies at home to post homework or assignments. Like minority enrolment, poverty concentration of the school is related to teachers' use of technology for communicative purposes. For example, teachers in schools with lower poverty concentrations were generally more likely than teachers in the highest poverty schools to use computers or the internet to communicate with colleagues. Fifty-nine percent of teachers in schools with less than 11 percent, 55 percent of teacher in schools with 11 to 30 percent, and 54 percent of teachers in schools with 31 to 49 percent of students eligible for free or reduced-price school lunch used these technologies at school for this purpose, compared with 38 percent of teachers in schools with 71 percent or more students eligible for free or reduced-price school lunch. Similarly, 53 percent of teachers in schools with poverty concentrations of 11 to 30 percent eligible for free or reduced-price school lunch used these technologies at home to communicate with colleagues, compared with 40 percent of teachers in schools with 71 percent or more students eligible for free or reduced-price school lunch.

Fifty-three percent of public school teachers indicated that they used computers or the internet for instruction during class time. Elementary teachers were more likely to do this than secondary teachers, and teachers in schools with smaller enrolments were more likely to do this than teachers in schools with the largest enrolments. Teachers in schools with lower minority enrolments were generally more likely to use computers or the internet for instruction during class time than teachers in schools with high minority enrolments. Similarly, teachers in the lowest poverty schools (based on percent of students eligible for free or reduced-price school lunch) were more likely than teachers in schools with 50 to 70 percent eligible students to use computers or the internet in this way.

Elementary teachers were more likely than secondary teachers to assign programmes using the computer *inside* the classroom, and less likely than secondary teachers to assign programmes using the computer *outside* of the classroom. Teachers' use of technology for instructional activities varied by a number of school and teacher characteristics. For example, elementary teachers were more likely than secondary teachers to assign students to use computers or the internet to practice drills. In addition, elementary teachers were more likely than secondary teachers to assign students to use these technologies to solve problems and analyse data. On the other hand, secondary teachers were more likely than elementary teachers to assign students to use these technologies to conduct research using the internet.

Teachers in schools with different enrolment sizes varied with respect to whether they assigned students to use computers or the internet for various instructional activities. Teachers in schools with smaller enrolments were nearly twice as likely as teachers in schools with large enrolments to assign students to use these technologies to practice drills. Teachers in schools with smaller enrolments were also more likely than teachers in schools with the largest enrolments to assign students to use computers or the internet to solve problems and analyse data. There were also differences in whether teachers assigned students to use technology for various instructional activities according to minority enrolment. For example, teachers in schools enroling the smallest proportion of minority students were more likely to assign students to use these technologies for word processing and creating spreadsheets than teachers in the highest minority enrolment schools.

Teachers in lower minority enrolment schools were also generally more likely than teachers in the highest minority enrolment schools to assign students to use these technologies for multimedia presentations and CD-ROM research. Finally, teachers in schools with smaller proportions of minority enrolments were more likely to use computers or the internet for internet research. Similar to the differences in minority enrolment, school poverty concentration is related to a number of activities for which teachers assign students to use computers or the internet. Teachers in schools with the lowest poverty concentrations were more likely than teachers in schools with the highest poverty concentrations to assign students to use these technologies for graphical presentations, multimedia presentations, word processing and spreadsheets, research using CD-ROM and the internet, and corresponding with experts.

Experimental Learning

Experiential, or experience-based learning can be regarded as the earliest approach to learning for the human race, the significance and potential of it has not been fully recognised until relatively recently. In the formal education system it has tended to be developed and regarded as somehow fundamentally inferior to those organised forms of knowledge which have been constructed as subjects or disciplines. The practical and the applied do not tend to have the same status in educational institutions as the academic and the abstract. Interestingly, scholars from outside of youth education often have a more sanguine contribution to make in defining how people learn.

Analysing Experiential Learning

Conceptual analysis as a technique is used by philosophers to analyse illusive phenomena. By asking "what" questions and relentlessly dissecting the answers until a residue can be identified, they attempt to reveal the truth about a phenomenon. The methodology employs a test known as the necessary and sufficient conditions test. In this instance, what would be the necessary and sufficient conditions for experiential learning to exist? Experiential learning was defined as learning which combined mental, emotional, and physiological stimuli. These necessary and sufficient conditions for experiential learning were organised and distilled from a range of individual and group responses. There must be a balance of aural, visual, tactile, olfactory, and emotional stimuli. Learning involves observing, doing, or living through things. Intrinsic motivation transcends extrinsic motivation.

— The learner, in some significant respect, is the initiator of the learning.

— The learning process, in some respect, is perceived to be controlled by the learner.

— The goals of the learning process, to some extent, are thought to be the learner's goals.

— Accountability for the learning act or actions is the perceived province of the learner.

Analysis and reflection are a significant part of the learning act, i.e., the learner values what he/she is learning and there is an extension to that learning. The nature of the learning process itself is such that it is often associated with objectivity, subjectivity, and open-endedness. There is sustainability and consistency associated with the learning. The conditions under which experiential learning were thought to exist by these teacher candidates are often contradictory to what is considered common knowledge about how children learn in school or how they should be taught. The belief that learning is a trial and error process provides one example. Children quickly learn in school that there are right and wrong answers to most questions.

Most knowledge is abstracted in such a way that it can be digested in small doses, avoiding knowledge about phenomena that are difficult to define or quantify. Yet beyond a fundamental base of knowledge or literacy/numeracy, living is very much a subjective trial and error process which requires a balance of factual and practical knowledge, much of which is about 'best' solutions, not right versus wrong answers. Most technologists and many technological education teachers know this general truth and apply it in their own learning/teaching.

Another way of defining something from first principles is to compare and contrast it with a phenomenon that it is not. This technique is referred to by scholars as comparative analysis. Comparative researchers will often begin their studies by setting up a juxtaposition then search for a unifying concept and hypothesis to illuminate it. Many technological education teachers have a life and work experience base from which to draw when designing learning activities in schools. More important, this base is much more central to the effectiveness of these teachers and to curriculum design generally than heretofore thought. Such teachers and the teacher educators who prepare them initially for the role of teacher would do well to ensure this aspect of professional life is valued and recognised more widely. In the context of increasing teacher accountability, reducing teacher control on a system-wide basis could be a recipe for disorder if not chaos. On the other hand, interests outside of and inside the schooling infrastructure are calling for greater relevance in the curriculum and an experiential curriculum could be the answer.

4

Online Learning

Rapid changes in technology are a challenge for schools and states trying to keep teachers up to date. Another challenge is teachers' lack of access to adequate equipment and software. For example, a teacher who participates in an e-mail training session needs to have the chance to use that new skill upon returning to the classroom. Training without access to equipment is a waste of time and money. InTech focuses on curriculum and teaching methods rather than starting with technical skills. Technology gradually is infused into training. Teachers participate in intensive workshops and contribute lesson plans that incorporate technology into the classroom to share with others in the program. Teachers also point to the lack of quality training in ways to integrate technology into the teaching process. There are few quality models demonstrating ways to integrate technology into the curriculum that can be used to build training programs for veteran teachers. As educators become more skilled with computer equipment, they need training in applying these skills in the classroom. Professional development in technology until recently has reflected 'one size fits all' thinking, and training has focused on broad technical skills rather than specific uses for technology in the classroom. However, teachers of different grade levels or subjects have different needs for technology training. A first-grade teacher may use a computer to help reinforce students' reading skills. But a high school science teacher needs to use specialized equipment and software to conduct experiments in the classroom and spreadsheets to gather and analyze the data collected.

Online Teaching Tools

During the period 1992, saw the beginning of the World-Wide Web. The Internet stands for 'internetworking', i.e. when two or more computers are internetworked allowing for communication between them. It is now taken to relate to the global network that allows you to send a message to a machine elsewhere on the network, in this case a global one, or to look at information on a remote machine. There is no Internet as such. It is made up a series of Wider Area Networks (e.g. JANET) talking to each other, which in turn are made up of Local Area Networks (e.g. the network for an individual University), i.e. networks within networks. The Internet provides academics with an opportunity to make their teaching better, to allow them to teach in different ways to the standard one-to-many lecture, and to reach more students. Simply put, it allows for the 'maximisation' of learning. In other words the Internet allows for a more efficient and interesting way of 'imparting knowledge'. To add to this, the Internet (and most notably the Web) can display the following advantages. In most cases it is:

— cheap
— easy to use (as both an author and a learner)
— fashionable
— attractive to students
— cross-platform
— suitable for accessing resources of various media
— ideally suited for remote learning, i.e. 'remote' from the classroom either by location or time
— interlinking providing access to resources held in other subject areas and institutions
— suited to increasing collaborative work and cross-institution communication

Traditionally the Internet seemingly provides two options. The first 'is a form of distance learning in which a tutor places courseware on a Web server where it can be accessed by remote students' identifying the disadvantages of such a system as being expensive if one is to insure 'enough software to meet the demands of a complete syllabus'. Alternatively there is the 'independent study in which learners search the Internet for materials that are relevant to their interests'. Again this has disadvantages most notably because the suitability of the material students access cannot be guaranteed. Internet Based Learning (IBL), learner is provided with access to courseware stored on the campus or the Internet from either location'. A successful teaching model could involve then 'orientating, motivating, presenting, clarifying, elaborating, consolidating, and confirming'. This can be married with the pedagogical aims of such Internet-based projects as JTAP's COSE which outlines: A largely constructivist view is taken in that learning is seen as an active process in which learners construct new ideas or concepts based on their existing knowledge and skills, but it is considered that for true learner autonomy to be achieved a structured development of essential learning skills is also required. These learning skills include:

— procedural skills

— knowledge/memory skills

— mental agility

— problem solving skills

— time management

— learning management

— organisational skills

The evaluation of the new technologies for educational purposes implies that the Internet does work as an effective teaching tool but only if certain rules have been observed. As well as obeying the standard guidelines for computer-aided learning (e.g. a good user interface, effective navigational tools, etc.)

Along with life-long learning, one of the most over-used expressions at the moment is that of 'resource-based learning' or 'RBL'. Simply put, this focuses on the concept of giving the learner greater access to resources (and thus more control of their learning experience). Because of the multimedia and easy to access advantages of the Internet, the use of on-line teaching (especially with the widespread popularity of the Web) has led many to advocate the policy of marrying the two together. There is no simple answer to this, as it depends entirely on the teaching goals of the course, and the technological capability of the host institution. As a guide, however, it can be looked on as a straight forward trade-off: increased virtuality (i.e. more technically advanced uses of the Internet) means more work required for setting up the course and insuring its success. For example, it is very easy and quick to set up an e-mail list, but it is far more complicated to run a MUD (Multi-User Dungeon).

E-rate Programme

In United States, the Federal Communications Commission decided to increase funding for the E-rate programme to ensure the even distribution of education technology. Before the E-rate Programme, only 39% of classrooms in poor school districts had Internet connections while 62% of classrooms in wealthier districts did. In just the first year, the E-rate program has lowered the cost of telecommunications services for over 80,000 schools and libraries and helped more than 38 million children. Forrester Research credits the E-rate program with increasing Internet access for African-Americans and Hispanics. At the new funding level, 528,000 public school classrooms will be wired to the Internet providing new tools for 40 million American students.

The E-rate program gives priority to the neediest schools and libraries based on the household incomes of students' families. Although 89% of public schools have some Internet access today, only 51% of the nation's classrooms are connected. Only 39% of classrooms in high-poverty areas are connected—compared to 62% of the classrooms in wealthier areas. Low-income and minority households are the least likely to be participating in the telecommunications revolution. The E-rate program is working to ensure that the children of these households have access to the information tools they will need to master to participate in economy and be prepared for the growing percentage of jobs that require technology literacy. If American students cannot fill these jobs, they will fill them with foreign workers, a growing trend of the last few years. The Digital Education Act of 1999 would amend title III of the Elementary and Secondary Education Act of 1965 to provide for digital education partnerships. The Act would make available $25 million for grants to develop, produce, and distribute educational and instructional video programming that is designed for use by kindergarten through grade 12 schools.

These Digital Education Content Collaboratives would include public television stations, state departments of education, local education agencies, businesses, and colleges and universities. The content would be formatted to take advantage of new digital broadcasting capacity and school computer and server infrastructure. To successfully integrate education technology into the classroom, define more clearly what intellectual skills students need, and develop better techniques for teaching them. Many educators believe that efforts to wire the schools need to accompanied by new approaches to curriculum development as well. Both teachers and students need to be equipped with new skills and intellectual tools that will enable them to critically engage the information technologies that are quickly becoming an integral part of school infrastructure. In general, the E-rate has been "effective at doing what it was intended to do."

The best sites are those where there is constant support for teachers within the schools. Where there is an entrenched system of educational technology in place. This means that there is on site teacher training, maintenance, and a place and time for colleague sharing. The Gateway currently contains 6,672 education resources. Sponsored by the Department of Education's National Library of Education, the Gateway is a special project of the ERIC Clearinghouse on Information & Technology. The NEA is also helping to prepare teachers for teaching in the Information Age though programs of the National Foundation for the Improvement of Education. The NFIE provides grants and technical assistance to aid teachers best utilizing rapid changing modes of learning. Two past grant programs were exclusively focused on professional development in the area of educational technology: Traditional theory says that kids need to know discrete skills in computation or reading so that's what teachers teach. That's what's expected and they come to think that's their job. But most of the people who are excited about technology in schools don't believe that's what it's about. They generally care more about having kids do sophisticated writing or engage in complex reasoning or learn to figure things out like adults do. The ideal of classrooms linked to the outside world will make sense only if students can find supportive communities when they venture electronically beyond their classrooms. Technology is giving parents, businesses, nonprofit organizations, governments, and others an enormous opportunity—and responsibility—to become more involved in educating children.

Many citizens and communities answered this opportunity by participating in NetDays—grassroots volunteer efforts to wire schools so they can network their computers and connect them to the Internet. Labor and materials come from volunteers and support from companies, unions, parents, teachers, students, and school employees. Massachusetts, at the state level, is making commitments to connect schools with the rest of their communities. Through the Massachusetts Community Network (MCN), the state will select a private vendor to provide inexpensive, high-speed data communications services, including Internet access, to public schools, public libraries, municipal offices and state agencies.

Open Learning Communities

The information and communication technologies (ICTs), dramatically expand options for engaging in teaching and learning at the individual, community, and societal levels. ICTs provide opportunities for greater flexibility, interactivity and accessibility. They help visualize applications such as interactive radio and television, videoconferencing, teletext, Internet-based environments of dialogue, web publishing, and individualized CD-ROM tutorials. Discussion around these new technologies thus tends to stir up a whole range of emotions ranging from optimism and hope to uneasiness and anxiety. The reason for this is that, in addition to expanding current delivery options, the emergence of these new technologies present us with the opportunity to question fundamental assumptions, to re-think existing approaches, to collectively conceptualize and generate new ideas and community-based alternatives and even sometimes, albeit more rarely, to catalyze social and institutional change. However, to unlock the potential of such technologies, it is critical to revive an age-old discussion over means and ends. Technology, however sophisticated and inspiring to the imagination of technologists, will not automatically result in the benefits that are sometimes forecast by its advocates.

The history of technology shows a disappointing repetition of instances of predicted revolutions that subsequently failed to materialize. In the majority of these cases of stunted growth, the attention to the means overshadowed the concern with the ends. The pursuit of ever more hi-tech forms of technology and increased access to technology can only be justified by expectations about their potential contribution to a better world. Just chasing after the hottest technologies is a shallow pursuit and not worth the excitement it often generates. The overriding questions are: What are goals, how do these goals relate to creating a better world, and how do the technologies pursue help achieve goals? In the domain of education, a greater level of complexity surrounds these questions. Not only are the emerging technologies affecting the means by which facilitate learning, they are also influencing the ends themselves. There is an intimate link between developments in the world of learning and those that pertain to the information society.

This relationship will be analyzed in more detail in the sections that follow. The learning side of the equation will be tackled first. Two perspectives will particularly be highlighted: the recognition that learning is an innate ingredient of very humanity and the ensuing concern that conventional learning environments are not well-suited for meeting society's learning objectives. Learning is taking on a distinctly enhanced meaning. It is a time when changes in the learning environment, which have been advocated for decades if not centuries, are becoming necessary rather than merely desirable. Learning is an essential basis for both action and reflection and thus for creativity and problem solving.

Learning is a pursuit in its own right which goes beyond the utilitarian conceptions that have for a long time related it almost exclusively to the world of work. In developing and industrialized nations alike, change, and consequently the need to respond and adapt to change and to manage ensuing conflict, are fundamental ingredients of life. Learning is the mechanism through which human beings cope with — and in turn contribute to — change. The possibility to engage in learning throughout one's life and across multiple dimensions of life is thus essential for survival as well as a condition for continual quality of life. The traditional perceptions regarding education, based on the assumption that learning is the prerogative of the young, and that adult learning is at worst a response to failure and at best a marginal supplement, an exception rather than the rule, are becoming rapidly outdated.

Learning is increasingly seen as a lifelong and life-wide requirement. This is contrary to the notion of learning as a mere preparation for life — with a discrete beginning and end — but not as an integral part of life. To be a productive and participating member of society, one needs to be able to continue to learn, to grow with changes in the environment and to respond to the availability of different opportunities. For example, the increasing emphasis on informal sector activities as well as changing patterns of employment cause linear career paths to be replaced by career networks in which people find themselves exploring distinct environments and moving into divergent directions at various stages of their lives. Inherent in the emergence of the information society is also the need to rethink the priorities accorded to work-related activities vis-à-vis activities not directly related to the world of work. This is particularly relevant considering that in many societies people now spend decreasing proportions of their active life on what traditionally would be called 'work' and increased proportions of it on activities that would traditionally have been seen as pertaining to 'leisure.' Quality of life, then, becomes less a function of self-realization in the (formal and informal) work environment and more a dimension of, for instance, social, cultural and political participation in society.

The boundaries between work, leisure and learning start gradually to disappear and learning becomes a dimension of a work/learning/leisure merger. Learning for work, learning for leisure, and learning for learning are all valid options within that context. The above conceptualization requires us to rethink traditional learning goals, such as literacy. Literacy has long been seen as a gateway to the world of learning. However, its definition as the ability to describe and interpret the world in terms of alphanumeric symbols is no longer adequate. There are many literacies and, consequently, illiteracies.

Technological illiteracy, political illiteracy, ecological illiteracy, intercultural illiteracy, and so many other ways in which people are hindered in their ability to act and reflect upon their environment are just as important as the inability to read and write. Across these various literacies there is a growing problem of information overload which threatens to paralyze us. The inability to process and critically analyze information is increasingly a concern. Learners must develop the ability to access and process huge volumes of information so as to create meaning and generate new knowledge. The world has known unmet learning needs as long as education has been a conscious concern of societies. What is new now is that such unmet learning needs can no longer be seen as isolated phenomena within the boundaries of particular countries or distinct parts of the world.

The world is increasingly becoming a global society and a learning place in its own right. The extent to which the world will be able to learn, will condition its survival and its ability to make the planet an acceptable, and hopefully desirable, place to live. Global learning depends on the ability of societies to turn themselves into learning societies and of communities within societies to constitute themselves as learning communities. In turn, learning communities exist to the extent that their individual members are learning individuals. But what is the global reality? As we approach the end of the second millennium, there are still more than 900 million illiterate people in the world. New illiterates emerge every day as the result of inadequate school systems, inappropriate curricula, and insufficient conditions to prevent relapse into illiteracy once people have become literate .

More than 130 million school-age children world-wide do not go to school. The millions that do go to school often fall victim to the diploma disease, ending up with learning achievements that do not relevantly relate to their immediate needs nor guarantee that learning sustains throughout their lives. School systems, reflect the requirements of the formal economy and, besides their obvious role in serving the learning needs of new generations, they also serve as channels for the socialization of human beings into the pre-existing socio-economic hierarchies pertaining to the formal system. They are ill-equipped to respond to the learning challenges and opportunities of the future. Schools are burdended with a great deal of pressure due to increasing demand. In the past, they served a smaller and less diverse clientele, often already in many ways pre-selected.

Furthermore, many schools are weakened by outdated structures which constitute an impediment to learning. Among these barriers are the continued reliance on the artificial separations between levels of education, such as primary, secondary and tertiary, or between socio-economically biased different tracks of learning, such as academic and vocational or technical. Equally inappropriate are often the ways in which human knowledge has become compartmentalized in stale curricula and presented in ways that are relevant, if at all, only for portions of society. Furthermore, these curricula tend to narrowly concentrate only on a small portion of the intelligence spectrum. During the 1980's various researchers reviewed and broadened the concept of intelligence. Mainstream schools sometimes have difficulty in acknowledging other learning environments, other partners, or other systems of knowledge. They are furthermore limited — and are at great risk to rapidly grow almost totally out of touch with developments in society at large in often continuing to rely heavily on teachers as the main source of knowledge and information. With the changes taking place in society, schools are in dire need to de-formalize and re-constitute themselves as components of learning environments that facilitate people's mobility across a wide range of options to participate in society at large as well as in their local communities.

The world is changing at a scale and pace and with a level of interdependency to which are previously unaccustomed. This phenomenon of hyperchange is a combination of linear, exponential, discontinuous and chaotic change. Several forces, including the proliferation of information and communication technologies, the rapid production and flows of information, the globalization of fragile financial markets coupled with the parallel growth of informal local economies, the decentralization of governments and bureaucracies, the intense marketing of certain cultural fantasies and lifestyle preferences, and the rise of new political actors, are contributing to the intensifying, complexifying and churning of these change processes. The current global environment is filled with a great deal of tension, frustration and conflict that is closely linked both to real and perceived shifts in power, glaring inadequacies of 'modern' institutions that are being continually revealed, and a nagging uncomfortability which is tied to the inherent unpredictability and uncontrollability surrounding hyperchange.

The vision of a rational world order so eloquently articulated by the architects of the 20th century i.e., scientists, economists, and WWII statesmen, is becoming increasingly questioned in terms of both its achievability and desirability. Over the past three hundred years, the paradigm of modernity has played a significant role in shaping dominant notions of development, progress, growth, freedom, democracy, and social justice. However, several sacred intellectual spaces that have been closely linked to modernity are currently being contested and renegotiated on various terrains and at various levels of day-to-day lives. These challenged spaces include: the mechanistic/ reductionist views of systems vs. complexity, the objective vs. the subjective, the modern vs. the traditional, the universal vs. the culturally specific and pluralistic, the public vs. the private, the real vs. the virtual, the secular vs. the religious, the urban vs. the rural, individual vs. the community, the male vs. female vs. gender, the nation-state vs. the supra-national vs. local, and the individual vs. community.

Such contestations, on one hand, provide several reasons for optimism by opening up opportunities for shifting power and resources, generating new discourses and language, remapping borders, creating new identities, and liberating relationships. They also at the same, however, place tremendous pressure on the paradigm of modernity which can be expected to result in a multitude of skirmishes, shocks, bumps, dislocations, breaks, and ruptures as try to come to grips with a messy world. The levels of violence and destruction underlying these will no doubt be influenced by the global threats of militarization (further enhanced through increasing decentralization and commercialization of weapons), environmental degradation, and socio-psychological alienation. What should be viewed as particularly worrisome though is that the phenomenon of hyperchange places a severe strain on present abilities to make sense of, contextualize, adapt to, negotiate, and influence the opportunities and conflicts taking place around us. Many societies lack both relevant shared narratives and a respect for and understanding of other peoples' narratives. Many individuals and communities around the world today lack the ability to generate, link (the past, present and future), and evolve multiply interconnected personal narratives which provide them with a sense of meaning beyond themselves.

The ability to generate new meanings in socially constructive, pluralistic and non-violent ways can be seen to be constrained, to a large degree, by a breakdown of several social self-referencing mechanisms and feedback processes. A seemingly paralyzing inability to introduce, interact around and utilize new ideas. Anti-intellectual approaches masked under the rhetoric for 'pragmatism', 'practicality', 'implementation', and under false dichotomies of academic vs. practitioner and theory vs. action, are dramatically reducing the spaces for engaging in more critical, constructive and participatory forms of intellectual discourse which are essential for reflecting upon and challenging the ideological basis of how societies are being forced to conceive of their development. The results are the are unable to generate new visions to give context to ideas and new ideas to give greater context to visions. In addition, dominant analytical frameworks, methodologies, discourse, and interactions are not robust and dynamic enough to help us understand and respond in creative and diverse ways to the complex challenges that face the world. Yet, continue to attempt to construct mechanistic, first-order, single-discipline solutions to address these. Furthermore, most 'educated' people have been socialized to only see narrow immediate realities and isolated contexts which tend to be mired in the logic of functionalism, economic efficiency, cost-effectiveness, and risk averseness. Their ideas and positions are reduced to specific places, fixed periods of times, and rigid definitions of identity and social roles such as low caste, women, minority, left/ right, etc.

Such institutions are critical to enhancing awareness and consciousness, to continuously rejuvenating optimism and hope, and to supporting engagement in a process of radical transformation. However, having been simultaneously attacked by both the nihilistic forces of liberalism/post-modernism and preserved/hand-cuffed by the forces of conservatism , these spaces are either disappearing or becoming antequated and irrelevant. Many of surviving and emerging institutions prevent us from having the time to think about the different changes taking place around us and relationship to these. They also allow for dangerous levels of anonymity for the participants which has serious consequences for notions of social responsibility. Conventional notions of leadership have typically been framed in terms of those people who are in the elite ranks of governments, business, other organizations, rather than, in terms of all of us being leaders in different facets of lives. This has created a situation in which individuals are easily allowed to defer their personal responsibility for actions to the 'other.'

Many practiced models of leadership are still grounded in notions of authoritarianism and hoarding of power with the guiding metaphors of self-preservation and manipulation. Many of leaders have tended to adopt and hide behind positions based on the real-politik, partisanism and cynicism, and lack the courage and confidence to take bold risks in new directions. Preferring to preach dogma, they lack the ability to inspire others to create meaning in their lives. The crisis of meaning can be seen as being linked to the failures of modern education systems, and, more broadly, to limitations and biases of the dominant paradigm of development. The dialectical lifelong processes of discovery and self-realization, both on individual and collective levels, should serve to guide a much broader philosophy of learning which extends far beyond the conventional classroom and one-dimensional standardized tests. The responses to the crisis of meaning by the international development community have thus far centered around schooling with increasing calls for more 'basic education,' 'functional literacy,' and 'skills training' opportunities.

The critiques are by no means exhaustive and serve to highlight only certain concerns about the limitations of schooling. The extent to which this alphabet of generalizations applies to any particular context can, of course, be extensively debated. Positive examples can be found in the education system, but these occur in spite of the system rather than because of it. What should emerge from this discussion is that most educational systems today still remain insensitive to the widely diverse needs of learners of all age groups and ignorant to the complexity of learning processes. Furthermore, the institutionalized intervention of schooling has provided little space and empowerment for both individual learners and learner groups to engage in the construction of alternative visions of development.

Formal schooling, whether in person or at a distance, is an inappropriate solution by itself for dealing with the development challenges and opportunities of the future. Fullan , after extensive review of change initiatives, argues that introducing new innovations and reforms into current educational systems is "an ultimately fruitless uphill battle" as these systems have been designed to be resistant to change. He calls for "a new mindset about educational change." Thinking and acting in terms of open learning communities signifies a concerted effort to resituate means and ends in both education and in development—from a model of learning for development to learning is development. It represents an attempt to put into use and practice much of what already know.

The term 'open learning communities' is presented here in order to deliberately challenge the reader to think of learning beyond the conventional school-teacher-textbook modalities—to facilitate a shift from a culture of schooling to a culture of learning. The term should be seen as a symbolic descriptor representing the dynamic convergence of several ideological vectors (comprised of theories, movements, mini-revolutions, acts of resistance, and feelings of hope that are carriers of change) from around the world. Each particular open learning community can be seen to evolve out of specific cultural and historical processes, out of a response to a specific set of local/global problems, and out of dynamic interactions with its environment, other open learning communities and the contributions of the individuals who choose to participate in it. While there is no one pre-defined or pre-fabricated model of an open learning community, however, begin to articulate some principles (that are not fixed, but evolving) which contribute to envisioning open learning communities. To better explain the concept, the phrase will first be taken apart in order to lay out some of the key dimensions and implications of the terms 'open', 'learning', and 'community.'

Although this approach may appear to be a bit artificial or fragmentary, transforming the world of learning requires us to question and rethink the basic underpinnings of how see the world in terms of problems and opportunities, how engage in processes of learning, and how interact with each other. The phrase will then be re-assembled and discussed as a dynamic whole. As has been indicated, the vision of open learning communities is continually growing and evolving. The following exercise should therefore be viewed as an initial attempt to illustrate some key ideological vectors that are driving the notion of open learning communities rather than provide a precise comprehensive definition (which ultimately might prove to be counter-productive and restrictive). Others, of course, will have differing interpretations about the concept of open learning communities. It is therefore important that encourage such differences while at the same time, engaging in processes of dialogue centered around further elaborating, clarifying, sharing and reconfiguring certain understandings and frames of reference. The use of the term 'open' is strongly linked to processes of opening up the ways in which see and understand the world.

Open Thinking

Open thinking involves being able to see underlying structures and inter-relationships rather than linear cause-effect chains. It is closely linked to the notion of deep ecology which "sees the world not as a collection of isolated objects, but as a network of phenomena that are fundamentally interconnected and interdependent. Deep ecology (as distinguished from shallow ecology which is anthropocentric) recognizes the intrinsic value of all living beings and views humans as just one particular strand in the web of life". Within this context, there is a change in emphasis from viewing entities and organizational relationships in terms of hierarchical modes towards promoting more heterarchical linkages, i.e., systems in which each element is equally ruled by others. Open thinking involves the ability to shift analyses and reference points back and forth between different levels of systems (non-hierarchical systems nested within other systems) and across systems. It involves being able to move between different contexts and across different disciplines of knowledge. It also entails being able to connect different contexts and disciplines into more holistic frameworks.

Open thinking involves seeing change in terms of processes rather than as isolated snapshots. Such processes often take place in dynamic non-linear and unpredictable ways. This implies that willing to view conceptions of time differently. Time is conventionally perceived as being monochromatic in which events and acts follow in a certain definite sequence. Polychronic conceptions of time are used to describe different phenomena occurring simultaneously. Time is not understood in a linear way but rather as a set of certain points of mutual reference. Herman describes that, "Polychronic notions of time to a much larger degree admit the possibility of jump (qualitative) changes." Open thinking involves fuzziness—seeing the world in infinite shades of gray between black and white, not only in black in white terms. The fuzzy principle states that everything is a matter of degree. Fuzziness means multivalence i.e., three or more options, perhaps an infinite spectrum of options, instead of just two extremes. It is about living with contradictions: moving from a world of 'A OR not-A' to considering that 'A AND not-A' can both exist. Artificial divisions of formal, non-formal and informal education have little relevance as categories in isolation of each other. It calls for us to recognize that all live in "mediatized environments where education is simply one of many different cultural experiences". It asks that think in multichannel terms -- designing approaches based on understanding of the multiple channels that support different types learning processes and that learners engage in within a particular environment. This also involves discovering new ways to link these individual channels together. Within this context, it is important to understand how information flows between channels and environments and seek to stimulate different flows of information.

Open thinking also questions the value of using nation-states and geo-political borders as the primary unit of analyses for discussing learning systems. It pushes us to see institutions and policies in terms of horizontally and vertically overlapping layers ranging from the local to global. In addition, the idea of open calls for the introduction of more flexibility by moving away from constrictive and debilitating linear levels/ grades, divisions of education, and rigid time frames. The notion of open questions the value of using bivalent categories to describe complex realities such as: educated and uneducated, literate and illiterate, enrolled and unenrolled, developed and developing, rich and poor, modern and traditional, and so on. It pushes us to think beyond using isolated categories of race, class, gender. It strongly challenges the use of development strategies that target specific groups in isolation of each other such as out-of school and unemployed youth, drop-outs, street children, marginalized women, the poorest of the poor, unreached, etc.

Open also encourages us to think more holistically and moves away from highly compartmentalized and isolated disciplinary approaches towards more integrated frameworks. It encourages the building of linkages across sectors, for example, between learning, health, culture, politics and economics. It also requires that acknowledge the validity of other knowledge systems. There is a heterarchical space for a plurality of voices. Finally, the idea of open challenges us to look at work in development and education in terms of dynamic, continuous processes rather than as discrete projects which will result in easily definable end-products. The international development community must come to recognize that the future can neither be predicted nor manufactured. The notion of 'learning' is a very broad and multi-dimensional one. Learning has implications for how people search for, acquire, analyze, synthesize, use and share information and skills from a variety of media; how they perceive themselves, reflect on their condition and negotiate their identities; how they connect with others and their environments; how they seek to express themselves, grow, and develop their own capacities to continue to learn; and how they construct meaning and evolve their consciousness. Because of its inherent "ephemeralness and unpredictability" and the diversity of contexts in and purposes for which it takes place, learning is extremely difficult to describe. Rather than attempt to provide an extensive overview of learning, this part will merely serve to highlight a few aspects of learning that are particularly relevant to the concept of open learning communities.

There is a wide range of goals that exist for learning which are culturally, systemically and learner defined. A few goals which incorporate both individual and societal dimensions for why learn are discussed. Learn both for survival and in order to give greater meaning to lives.

These goals are also not seen as static and are given meaning through the interpretations of different communities and individuals which allows them to go beyond being words on a piece of paper. Within this context, there is an understanding that spaces must be provided for interacting around the goals of learning in a pluralistic and participatory manner, in which there is strong respect and value given to different belief systems, knowledge systems, cultural values, and languages. The goals of learning in terms of processes which provide for the varying cognitive, emotional, psycho-social, health and nutritional, moral/ethnical, cultural/artistic, technological, participation, ecological and spiritual needs of individuals and communities.

Within the framework of open learning communities, there is a conscious attempt to link understandings and lessons from the past and the present towards actively constructing the future. This implies creating contexts in which are expected to make mistakes and in which are encouraged to learn from mistakes. This also involves a shift in emphasis from status quo-based approaches which have supported maintenance learning. Rather, there should be a concerted effort to promote innovative learning which prepares individuals and communities to deal with "new situations through the integration, synthesis, and the broadening of horizons. Its meaning derives from dissonance among contexts. It leads to critical questioning of conventional assumptions behind traditional thoughts and actions, focussing on necessary changes. Innovative learning advances thinking by reconstructing wholes, not by fragmenting reality". Underlying the idea of innovative learning is the belief that learning involves interacting, meaning-making, reflecting and creating. In the context of open learning communities, learning is conceived of as a continuous, asynchronous lifelong process that individuals and communities engage in through a variety of experiences and interactions. Lifelong learning no longer refers simply to recurrent education or to a second chance for those who missed out in the first instance. Rather, it is a genuine lifelong endeavor, from the cradle to the grave.". The notion of learning challenges popular thinking which believes that learning is the prerogative and responsibility of the young. It argues that one is never too old to learn. Active learning can and does take place at all ages. The brain is remarkably plastic, constantly learning throughout the span of one's life.

Every human being can learn to be more intelligent. There are no longer categories of 'smart' and 'dumb' learners. All people can learn to become more effective, flexible and organized learners. What becomes important in this context is ability to continually develop the capacities to tap into potential. "The deeper meaning of learning to learn is associated with learners learning to extend and master their own capacities for learning". Learning to learn also calls for extending the notion of literacy beyond its functional definition to include multicultural literacy, technological literacy, democratic literacy, ecological literacy, critical media literacy, and so on. Each person develops a concept of 'self-as-learner.' Learning to learn involves developing oneself: to engage in critical reflection and creative thinking; to open up to other people's ideas, attitudes, and feelings; to become aware of and access learning resources through a variety of media; to recognize and question one's implicit assumptions; and to become less fearful of change. Learning to learn is also closely associated with processes that encourage us to think about learning. Metacognition is used to refer to an awareness of thought processes, and metamood is an awareness of one's own emotions. The term self-awareness reflects an ongoing attention to one's internal states. The capacity for self-awareness is directly linked to individuals becoming self-directed learners, taking responsibility for their own learning. Though all have the same set of physical systems, must begin to recognize and appreciate the diverse, complex, multifaceted nature of each human learner. Some of this difference is a consequence of genetic endowment. Some of it is a consequence of differing experiences and differing environments. The diversity is expressed in terms of personality and interests, cultures and family background, differing talents and intelligences, learning styles, motivation levels, and special needs. Vast ranges in diversity are characterize what it means to be fully human. Continually learning together is critical to building social relationships, negotiating difference and resolving conflicts. Approaches of collaborative learning and active participation are crucial in this process. Within the context of open learning communities, the notion of an omnipotent and omniscient teacher as 'expert' is strongly challenged. Classic roles around who is the teacher and who is the learner become mutated and enter into a perpetual state of flux. Learning is not a value-neutral set of processes. Learning is closely linked to different ideological positions and has political, cultural and socio-economic dimensions. The international development community, however, tends to discuss education as if it were something quite neutral. Very rarely, has this group been required to make explicit its ideological biases. The element of 'communities' is critical to consider as it constitutes the socio-cultural context for bringing individuals together to engage in shared meaningful experiences. Such interactions form the basis for learning and for becoming more fully human. It should be noted that there is no single generic, homogenous, universal community; rather, numerous types of communities exist throughout the world. Although this may seem to be an obvious statement, the international development community's discourse often fails to reflect this understanding as tend to use the term 'communities' to loosely refer to a widely divergent set of social groupings with different purposes, cultures, scales, etc. Recognizing the complexity and diversity of communities and their associated layers is important to supporting communities. There are alternative definitions of communities created for a variety of purposes, including those based on:

— geographic affiliations such as a village, rural district or urban areas;

— ethnic, racial, linguistic and religious groupings;

— sex and age;

— common occupations, interests, or experiences;

— a resistance to some outside force or threat;

— shared family concerns;

— a general shared philosophy.

Each community has its own peculiar identity which engenders its meaning, purpose, and intentionality and provides coherence around which system stability emerges. Communities are formalized in the sense that they do have some structure, a set of rules and logic to them, and several dimensions of culture. Communities also typically have several knowledge systems in parallel operation i.e., oral, public/private, male/female, religious, etc. and they are linked to different social, political, and economic institutions. Communities, however, have different sizes and boundaries. They are open in varying degrees to different types of information and people. Throughout the course of their lives, each individual participates in many different kinds of communities, with varying roles and objectives. A particular community is an evolving space in which the community's own identity and culture and that of its members is continually being defined, challenged, negotiated, and recreated by both its members and by other communities. Communities may emerge, evolve or collapse rather spontaneously through the unplanned interaction of many of dynamic and informal institutions and forces. There is an intimate link between learning and communities. Strong communities are important for learning, and learning constitutes an important process of building and linking communities.

Communities provide a humanizing setting for learning, which has been previously described as an inherently social activity. Communities provide an essential forum for making sense of the world, exploring and building natural historical and cultural ties, negotiating difference, drawing from and building moral and ethical frameworks, and creating development alternatives. Communities also provide the cultural specificity for situated learning. It is essential, however, that individuals be able to participate in different communities in order to develop different contextual frameworks. It is also important that efforts must be made to mediate and link the learning that takes place in different settings. In the context of open learning communities, a community must be a 'safe' space where learners can explore, share and grow.

Complex learning is enhanced by challenge and inhibited by threat. The brain/mind learns optimally—it makes maximum connections—when appropriately challenged in an environment which encourages taking risks. Positive emotions such as trust, love, tenderness and humor can facilitate learning. However, the brain/ mind 'downshifts' under perceived threat. It then becomes less flexible, and reverts to primitive attitudes and procedures. Negative emotions such as hostility, anger, fear, and anxiety can downshift the brain. This implies that a community must be 'personalized' rather than depersonalized i.e., looking at each learner as a special human being that belongs not numbers. Learning is also critical to creating new communities and linking them to one another. In recent times, there has been a great deal of romanticization around the notion of traditional communities. In discussing communities must not overlook the harsh realities that sometimes exist in many communities such as, resistance to new ideas and problems of unequal power relationships around race, class, gender, sexual preference, caste, age, etc. Nor, should ignore that communities are often formulated in exclusionary closed terms with membership being tightly controlled. Burnett adds that within communities, "conflict is inevitable and what families and communities learn to do is manage the conflicts to arrive at some measure of agreement, or even to more fully understand what divides them". Healthy communities are premised on both the individual and organization's ability to enter into dialogue and negotiate conflicts. Learning is the process by which begin to understand each other, to engage in different roles and relationships, to make sense of the conflicts around us, to see new opportunities for connection and create new identities. Learning is also about strengthening and evolving local knowledge systems and, at the same time, developing self-confidence in one's tradition, imagination, intellectual and organizations reserves.

The continued growth of such local knowledge systems coupled with the construction of critical frameworks for viewing other knowledge systems underlie the levels of creativity and sustainability of people-led development movements. Processes of learning are also critical to connecting communities to each other. Some communities have been created along more closed boundaries, other communities are sometimes hostile. By bringing in new energy and information and stimulating a process of dialogue, learning can be a force for opening up communities and facilitating meaningful gender-aware, inter-generational, and cross-cultural interactions within a community and across communities. When put back together, the energy and relationships inherent in open learning communities becomes much greater than simply the sum of its parts. The concept of open learning communities seeks to provide a dynamic alternative framework for seeing and acting in the world. The principle of self-organization implies the continual spontaneous emergence of diverse new communities and, at the same time, collapse of other communities. Within this context, every open learning community is a learning organism with its own evolving consciousness. Viewed as a complex adaptive system, the open learning community is constantly revising and rearranging its building blocks as it gains experience. It changes and adapt according to the divergent needs and interests of individual learners who participate and contribute to it as well as in response to the broader needs of society.

An open learning community must also continually reflect on itself in order to remain purposeful. Feedback loops enable a community to regulate itself, correct its mistakes, and re-organize itself. Such feedback loops are integrally linked to a process of being able to listen to voices from within and outside, to learn from them, and to allow the energies inherent in them to facilitate the process of social innovation and transformation. An open learning community is not only capable of adapting or even embracing change, it can generate change from within and can share this change with other open learning communities and their larger environment. In this sense, it is not simply a reactionary entity but rather a pro-active agent of change. Open learning communities should not be viewed as isolated parts. Rather, they should be seen as a set of relationships operating within a larger learning ecosystem. An important aspect of the learning ecosystem is that it optimally uses and distributes the intellectual, experiential, spiritual, and material resources available to it. Open learning communities within the same environment also influence and are influenced by each other. The flows of resources, information and energy form the basis for these relationships. Within this context, communities are continuously struggling with the tension of autonomy and differentiation vs. integration.

Each individual and community must seek to understand the ideological and practical implications for themselves and for others, as well as for the present and for the future. Such a process entails a fundamental shift in metaphor— from that of a book which is written and disseminated by the well-schooled elite to that of an interactive World Wide Web site that is constructed through more participatory and egalitarian methods. The focus of the shift, to clarify, is not on the medium; but rather, on the sets of attitudes, processes and relationships that surround the medium. The Internet has been described as a great democratizing force; a liberating and empowering tool. Under the metaphor of the Web site, there is a concerted effort to move from approaches of one-way dissemination to two-way sharing. Such a metaphor is geared around encouraging us to see ourselves as actively constructing and unfolding own vision of open learning communities, and linking it to the visions of others. Knowledge is seen as dynamic and evolving. The construction of the Web site constitutes a profound shared social experience—seen as something that the various participants build together. Furthermore, power over the process is transformed. Each one of us can contribute to and modify the vision of the site with text, pictures, sounds, videos can interact with each other around ideas; can hyperlink sites to other Web sites; even create own sites. However, be very aware that the medium of the Internet is not exempt from attempts at social control—efforts are currently being made by some institutionally entrenched actors to reproduce the metaphor of the book on the Internet. Engaging in processes of constructing the open learning community Web sites calls for a special set of attitudes and commitment. It will require that one be willing to move beyond fixing, defending, rationalizing or thinking solely in terms of the institution of schooling. It will mean exploring how to link learning back to the deeper social, political and spiritual problems that face world. It will require a commitment to enter into the often confusing and frustrating struggle of asking some basic philosophical questions—who are human beings, where are coming from, and where are going to. It will involve optimistic risk-taking—'a willingness to initiate fundamental processes of change, even when all of their implications are not known with total certainty in advance". It will ask that reconsider own privileged positions and the power structures to which derive authority from. It will require that open to experimenting with new ways of sharing and redistributing power.

The obstacles that stand in the way of envisioning open learning communities appear to be quite overwhelming. There are the vested interests of the educational establishment with its teachers' unions and textbook publishers and building contractors. There are the vested interests of the nation-state and resistance of politicians who are unwilling to make decisions which might jeopardize their political power. There are also the vested interests of the development industry which continue to see certain countries and groups as 'developed' and delinked from the problems of the South, and are fundamentally unwilling to challenge this deficit approach. Finally, there is the loosely aligned vested interests of modernity which rely heavily on the institution of schooling to reproduce its ideological frames of reference and socio-economic relationships. These various interest groups threaten to crush the concept of open learning communities. The world is a dynamic place where new discoveries are continuously being made, new institutions and relationships being formed, new opportunities are emerging.

Teachers' Role

The teacher is someone who intervenes in the learning process of others. The process can be seen as providing prompts for engaging, stimulating, structuring, and encouraging learning in individuals and communities. While transmission of some types of knowledge and skills is part of this process and will continue to be important, the complexity of society and demands made on the problem-solving capacity of human beings will require that teaching be seen as fundamentally going beyond the transmission of information. In the world of the future, envision that the teacher will be responsible for carrying out several inter-connected roles, as briefly described below.

— Facilitating learning entails building, accessing and validating a variety of activities, frameworks, information, and experiences for the learner to connect to. It should be clarified that facilitation implies more than simply providing access to new information or technologies; rather, it involves enabling understanding and creating meaning. This means raising the capacity of learners to ask questions rather than focusing on the provision of answers to predetermined questions. The teacher must challenge the thoughts and ideas of learners and stimulate them to engage in critical thinking and self-reflection. Essential to the process of facilitation is the ability of the teacher to link the appropriate set of interactions with the individual learning styles, interests and experiences of each learner as well as with the profiles of the communities that the learners perceive themselves as being part of.

— *Curriculum Innovation*: Centralized curricula around the world have often been unable to take into account the rich diversity in society and suffered from lack of imagination, flexibility and relevance.

The result is that many learners find themselves "lost" in the learning process. Given the broad range of learning styles, needs, interests, backgrounds, and aspirations of learners, teachers must adapt and develop new curricular approaches, content and language to ensure that curricula are, on one level, linked to the daily life of the learner but, on another level, push the learners to.8 explore beyond the mundane aspects of their daily lives into undiscovered possibilities. The movement towards decentralization provides an opportunity for allowing teachers greater control over the curricula. However, with curriculum innovation, there must be greater efforts to conduct decentralized and participatory field research in order to understand the strengths and weaknesses of different strategies. Engaging in such research allows teachers to interact constructively and flexibly with the curriculum on a continual basis.

— *Connection of Learners and Communities*: While learning is an individualized effort, it is also a social activity. Teaching must be conceived of in terms of a larger social exercise of connecting learners to each other and to the world around them. The process of connecting learners involves creating dialogue among diverse groups of learners that allow them to understand and appreciate the differences as well as the similarities that bond us as human beings. This means that teachers must be committed to understanding their learners and the communities that they come from. As part of this on-going process, they must also be willing to question their own internal biases and stereotypes.

— *Complementing/Supplementing Other Channels*: In addition to the traditional teacher, many other additional 'channels' currently exist and are emerging, such as textbooks, newspapers, and magazines, educational radio or TV broadcasts, computers, audio or video tapes, the surrounding physical and human environment, libraries, specialized work areas such as to perform science experiments or for creative expression. Teaching becomes a process of integrating these resources so that they complement, supplement and enhance each other. This demands a sensitivity to the inherent strengths and weaknesses of each of the channels and how they satisfy to different styles of learning and different types of content. Teachers can also play a role in introducing these new media into communities where there is often fear or resistance to change.

— *Motivational Support:* The teacher must play a critical role in providing motivational support through constructive feedback and encouragement to the learner, responding to a broad range of motivational needs .that vary over time and across learners. Learning is a process that is filled with success and failure—oftentimes involving great struggle and perseverance on the part of the learner. In many cases, failure can lead to great disappointment and withdrawal. However, if well managed, failure can also be turned into an important prompt to learning and thus can become the basis for success. It is the role of the teacher to provide positive inspiration at critical junctures of the learning process to ensure that learners stick with the laborious task of learning. However, the teacher should not take on this role in isolation, but rather seek to build a learning community in which other learners provide motivational support to each other as well.

— *Learning*: A good teacher is a continual learner. In order to be effective, the teacher must remain connected with changing societal frames of reference (economic, cultural, political, social, technological, etc.) as well as with changing needs and interests of learners. They must be able to learn from their environment. But more importantly, they must be able to learn from their learners. This involves constantly trying to understand how learners react to, interpret and create meaning from different activities. It also involves a willingness to experiment with and adapt new approaches. In addition, the process of teaching involves modeling a love of learning. This love is something that one cannot fake. If the teacher demonstrates a dedication to learning, there is a high probability that the learners will 'catch' that spirit of learning.

The teacher in the institution call 'schools' still has an important role to play in supporting the learning process. However, seek to break down the barriers that have supported the historical isolation of teachers in schools from other "teachers" in society. In order for continuous learning to occur, the responsibility for teaching must be distributed and integrated with other institutions and individuals in throughout society.

Learning is a natural human process that occurs wherever human beings interact with each other and with their environments. Much of society's effort to create the conditions for learning concentrate on the school system. However, learning can take place in formal as well as informal settings. It is not uncommon that some of the best instances of learning occur outside a formal setting as the learners tend to be more at ease and learning tends to be more contextualized within a relevant socio-cultural setting. For learning both within and outside the formal context to become optimally effective, it is thus important that artificial barriers between the two environments be reduced. Different media can play an important role in bridging the gap. The area of teacher education provides a natural starting point for initiating this process of change. However, as will highlight hereafter, it should be clear from the onset that teacher education is an integrated part of a broader conception encompassing the education of both learners and teachers for their new roles in open learning communities. In this section, then, we will discuss points of intervention into teacher education, particularly focusing on how information and communication technologies can be used to facilitate the process of change. But first it is necessary to reframe a few key conceptions around teacher education. The emergence of new ICTs provides an opportunity and a necessity for pursuing this exercise.

The distinction between pre-service and in-service education is no longer a useful one. This is particularly the case if begin to conceive of teacher education in terms of a more continuous and fluid process. In this context, pre-service teacher education is best to be seen as a preparation not only for a pre-determined role as teacher but particularly also for effective interaction with a continued learning-teaching process. The new ICTs help negotiate a hybridization between formal and distance education so that face-to-face teaching is no longer only for the pre-service education and distance education is no longer only reserved for in-service education. Throughout the teacher education process, there should be a strong integration of both face-to-face and distance learning approaches.

'Teacher/learners', as they emerge from their traditional roles, must now first of all learn to become good learners. Being a good learner is not an easy task — it requires a great deal of discipline, patience, resourcefulness, inquisitiveness, open-mindedness, creativity and flexibility. This implies that teacher education must put greater emphasis on developing in "teacher/learners" the skills required to become better learners. In addition to encouraging teachers to become learners, teacher education must also support the process of "learner/teachers" in becoming teachers, both in terms of how they can teach each other and how they can teach the teacher. Thus, teacher education may seek to involve "learner/teachers" in parts of the process. The new ICTs must not be viewed as replacing the human element in teacher education. There is increased frustration with the existing process of teacher education.

ICTs are sometimes seen as a means of 'fixing' this problem, particularly as they allow bypassing — or doing away altogether with — the assumed weak link, the traditional teacher trainer. This view, however, is erroneous. In a context of different media, including the human being as one of them, the most striking characteristic which distinguishes the human medium from non-human ones, is the capacity to learn. 'Teacher/ learners' can thus best be prepared for their new roles in an environment which models the behaviours they are expected to acquire. Such an environment should therefore be profoundly human and humanizing and technologies need to be incorporated in it so as to enhance, rather than to detract from, this human aspect. Many attempts at improving the quality and motivation of 'teacher/learners' through teacher training schemes have resulted in disappointment. Evaluations point, among other weaknesses, to the cascade model and its inherent transmission loss as well as to the gap between what is learned in the training situation and the realities of the field.

The use of information and communication technologies within a distance learning context is often advocated as a way to overcome such weaknesses. Excitement has been generated around new ICTs as it is assumed that they can 'bring the best expert directly to the teacher' and facilitate two-way communication between the teacher and learner. Unfortunately, these are very narrow applications of the ICTs and we do not foresee them to result in any significant shifts in learning and teaching as they are simply extensions of existing approaches and processes. These 'benefits' only serve to reinforce the teacher-over-learner hierarchies. However, the ICTs, if properly applied, possess the ability to unleash revolutionary changes in the field of teacher education.

Community Education

During 1970s, International Community Education Association (ICEA) which was founded, whose goal is to promote the concept of Community Education and help form a working network of worldwide initiatives. Today ICEA is represented in some 90 countries, accredited by the Council of Europe, and has operational relations with

UNESCO. Community Education stands for learning in the community, with the community, and for the community. It is to be understood as an integrating element of urban, community, and regional development efforts, contributing to the construction and reconstruction of economic infrastructure, cultural vitality and diversity, ecological consciousness and structural forms. Community Education serves to expand individual and communal responsibility aimed at taking action for the improvement in the quality of life. Hence Community Education means interventional learning in the Polis, and assumes that learning persons are also active social, economical, ecological, and political beings. The relationship between teachers and learners becomes a different one. Possibilities for an education towards entrepreneurship arise here, allowing people to take economic initiatives instead of only referring them to the nonexistent aid from agents of conventional control. Orientation towards the community, opening places of learning to the social environment, understanding the learning process as a part of local development, the connection between learning and community development in general: Community Education is not 'pedagogy' in the classical sense, but rather an active discourse and participation in complex realities.

The idea of Community Education has many years of broad practical experience behind it. But the knowledge gained could hitherto hardly be made available for scholarly systematization and theoretical development. Key problems such as the process of empowerment or ethnically strong communities in their struggles with the conflict between tradition and modernization have up to now been too little considered in the light of Community Education. However this does not change the fact that exactly these topics are those that have proven to be crucial in practice, as well as providing a focus in the theoretical development of innovative pedagogy and the comprehension of psychosocial processes. Community Education has taken diverse forms worldwide, with reference to different sources in the history of thought. The opportunities offered by Community Education to relate learning processes directly to actual problems in real-life situations, and thereby combine reflection and action with each other in a meaningful way, often harbour certain dangers, considering the overall contextual constraints which Community Education has to deal with, especially in the socioeconomic peripheral regions. Curtailment in practice is one danger. Others include programs dominated by conventional pedagogical measures (such as a frontal classroom for illiterates), as well as whole institutions which serve more as retreats for pedagogues escaping reality than as point of departure for engaging pedagogical activity in unprotected terrain, can also turn into aberrations on the educational landscape. There is neither a universal definition nor a well-developed theory of Community Education.

On the contrary, the analysis of the diverse developmental directions of this approach, its theoretical references and practical implementations, demonstrate that there is a kind of agreement on a number of central principles which form the basis for a pedagogical, educational, and sociopolitical orientation of Community Education and for the design of life and learning processes. Such principles include for instance a holistic approach, life-long learning, empowerment, participation, help towards self-help, community development, decentralization, the networking of different areas of life and learning as well as of institutions and resources, and a cross-generational, multi-topical, interdisciplinary cooperation and partnership. The demand for Community Education is growing worldwide. This quantitative development has brought with it a large store of on-site experience. Characteristic of the hitherto weak infrastructure of the movement, however, is the lack of comparative culturally sensitive documentation and archiving of such experiences. Related to this fact is the concomitant lack of theoretical development on the phenomenon. The theory deficit on the one hand and the diverse, often undesired limitation of Community Education on the other hand make it clear that Community Education is a concept that needs to be elucidated. By nature, Community Education crosses borders. For educators and pedagogical scientists, this invaluable access to reality provides a largely yet unprocessed challenge.

Community Education deals with de-schooled learning, which can certainly be promoted when institutions of the formal educational system become more open to the outside world. Nevertheless, contradictions between educational processes more strongly subjected to didactic reduction, and learning and experiencing procedures in the sense of Community Education, are in fact part of the educational landscape of many countries. Community education is not easy to introduce, since it challenges existing professional and administrative hierarchies and cuts right across the different domains. In its developmental stage it is not a panacea for all ills but may even add to the complexity of social development processes and procedures. Yet, once beyond this developmental stage, when it has demonstrated its principles and shown its implementation possibilities, its rationale becomes clear and leads to the realization of its aims and objectives. The following distinguishing features of Community Education emerge as important:

— Community education is a holistic approach which supports the learning in, with and for the community. It counts on self-reliance, mobilizes the power of communities and focuses them on sustainable development, on the solution of social, cultural, technological, economic and ecological problems. All the social and all the age groups of the population can be involved. That is why community education overcomes the separatism of 'hyphen-pedagogies', when the project allows it; it is more than just adult education or vocational training. It works in an integrating way.

— The key problems and situations of the people in the community are the starting point of the learning process. The search for local alternative forms of energy can become a contribution to prevent global climatic changes. Many local problems (with their global aspects) cannot be solved without the supporting approach or community education. This is true for family planning just as much as for dealing with natural resources in a responsible way.

— Community education is never just education, but always organization and action as well. Thus the application of acquired knowledge and abilities in complex real-life situations becomes an integral part of the learning process. Not only is the subject the point of concentration, but also the situation that should be dealt with and improved. That is why community education never just aims at the qualification of people, but also at a constructive dealing with the reality in which these people are living.

— Community education is especially sensitive and responsible with regard to the living conditions of marginalized ethnic groups. It supports social movements that aim at overcoming this marginalization. It makes an effort for full equal rights of women. It promotes the realization of human rights, the integration and acceptance of ethnic, cultural or religious minorities, it has an intercultural and antiracist orientation. It becomes active against the isolation of handicapped people.

— Community Education and popular economics work together in many cases. From the beginning ICEA has seen and emphasized the importance of economics from below as a way out of marginalization. Here ICEA above all emphasizes the promotion of entrepreneurship. For where there is a lack of jobs, people have to be able to create jobs themselves. ICEA supports those, often from the informal sector, who want to get access to the regular market.

— Community education is an answer to specific weaknesses of institutions and curricula in the formal educational sector. Learning as participation in sustained development does not need any artificial motivation. It is easier to put new insights into reality. Academic knowledge is used for concrete problems and not taught in an alienated form. Knowledge and abilities can be acquired in a process of investigating learning with a close connection of theory and practice.

— Community schools are referring to local needs with their curriculum, they reconstruct the relationship to the neighbourhood and lead children and adolescents at an early point and more intensively than traditional schools to social fields of action. This also outlines the paradigm of community education in contrast to conventional educational approaches:

— Learning processes are not cut up into meaningless units and placed beyond reality. Community education lays emphasis on holistic learning in meaningful connections. Technical qualifications with instruments are learnt in an enlightened social context. Learning does not take place in parameters of phony security where tasks, the method of solving the problem and the solution are all known beforehand. Instead, learning takes place in the uncertainty of complex reality. People learn in a close theory-practice correlation. Community education favours the inquiring and discovering type of learning -learning through productive action.

— Community education emphasizes development of the curriculum from the bottom up instead of the top down. Subjects do not structure it but key situations and key problems. Their analysis makes the classification of desirable qualifications possible which allow autonomous, competent action and solidarity. The connection with key situations initiates learning processes close to reality and a focus of scientific knowledge on real problems.

— Community education contributes to an opening of educational institutions to social action fields without being fixed to educational institutions. Here it is accepted that important social learning processes take place - especially under conditions of marginalization -beyond the walls of educational institutions.

— Community educators are not shaped by white-collar convictions, they do not migrate from the land and they do not rely on teacher-proof curricula. They interpret learning as an active participation in local and regional development. They combine brain-work with manual work.

Open Learning Community would mistake their role if they did not become critical and simultaneously constructive adversary of only pragmatic variants of Community Education; the development of standards of excellence is necessary right there, where due to their existential situation, people cannot afford to grind through an examination-ridden curriculum alienated from reality. Community Schools promote cross-generational learning in many project forms. Looking around in the classrooms in the morning, one can find housewives, unemployed people, and workers in their free shift, all who join the young people there studying for their O or A-levels in Geography or Physics. In the evenings and on weekends one finds young people and adults alike, attending classes together in computer technology, law, or auto repair, or pursuing common hobbies such as body building and yoga.

Tolerance is the prerequisite for the British variant of Community Education. Nothing is smoothed over here, no special paths paved; everyone is admitted, and if need be the matter is discussed. Hence old women and men practicing folkdances meet up with punkers who are going to a karate class.

Poor children cannot afford childhood. Millions of them live on the street and care for themselves, sleeping in doorways or under bushes. They work on their own accounts or illegally in factories. They cope with corrupt police and know how to sweet-talk customers. They help each other and pay protection money. They form gangs and hunt for prey. They perform self-justice and have pity. They develop their own toys. They sell bananas and drugs, newspapers and chiclets; they harvest cotton, clean shoes, and carry rocks. Life for them is filled with risk, for they could die of parasites, beatings, or starvation. Yet at the same time it is replete with adventure, better than the grimmest hut that can never be a home or the dull prison of welfare. The children of the Third World are more capable than the children of invented childhood. Productive Community Schools could mean 1000 colourful flowers, 1000 variations and attempts to acquire extensive experience through the realization that school should not cause the children of the poor to lose their entrepreneurial skills. Instead it should start at the point they have already reached on their own. The International Community Education Association has provided 5000 dollars of start-up funds for both schools.

A Community School networks with other external learning venues, builds satellites, works on projects with other non-school groups and institutions. It works against segregation, and against the splitting of young and old, domestic and foreign, handicapped and non-handicapped, inner life and outer world. Its teachers are not only teachers but also community developers. Important chances of retaining the relationship between schools and community were simply gambled away, and the potential uses of schools as learning and experiencing centres on a larger scale basically ignored.

An Open Learning Community is a broad concept embracing a network of groups and institutions which come together for a certain purpose, pursue a common goal, and attain knowledge in the process. There are plenty of cases in which this has occurred without the participation of either pedagogues or money-providing institutions to trigger the process. An Open Learning Community does not automatically arise because people and institutions have been stimulated to work and learn together as much as possible. A generative topic is needed, some issue that truly touches people in their own lives. A problem cannot be artificially "planted", it must be either latently or manifestly present. In joint learning processes, in combining reflection with action, the chance has to be recognized and grasped to develop strategies for problem solving that involve intervening in situations to work for the improvement of those involved. A situation and problem analysis of some sort is necessary, carried out in discussion with those affected. A theory or approach to the situation or problem must be developed, in order to begin applying attempted solutions at strategic points. There are a whole series of possible methods which can be used in clarifying the relationships involved. The generative core stimulates the learning and development process when it represents an actual problem complex consciously recognized by someone involved. It generates goals, activities, and mutual duties of those learning. This analysis completes a "participatory research", in which in principal all those participating in a situation can be involved. Such research is to be equated with an intervention in reality.

The chance of initiating an Open Learning Community depends largely on whether generative topics or key problems of considerable existential importance can be identified or not. If they are lacking, even the most committed pedagogues will first grind out their teeth on the apparent mental immobility of their potential clientele before they can create an educational movement without a true motive Community Education/ Educación Popular found new backing here and became a part of the ferment instigated by these movements. Teachers need partners, they need an alliance with other social forces to prevent their clientele from smashing vainly into hard walls which cannot be overcome. It doesn't have to be social movements, it could also be NGO's, companies, or municipalities.

Longer-term projects towards Open Learning Communities require a stable backing. This can be ministries, to the extent they themselves are capable of at least mid-term stable planning. Ministries with relatively high fluctuation rates not only on the top of the political ladder, but often in the entire staff as well, are only of limited use, as a great deal of experience has demonstrated. If one turns to NGOs one must first check whether they are built on strong foundations, and do not resemble Potemkin villages which only simulate a real existence when financial contributions appear on the horizon. An Open Learning Community here means entering into dialog with the families living in the region, responding to their key problems (such as the acquisition of fuel and building materials or the search for additional sources of income), developing and promoting awareness of the relationships between tree-cutting and the pending ecological-economic disaster, and recruiting children as well as parents as vital supporters of a reforestation project.

The basic methodology is linked to the situational approach combined with the theory of traumatic processes. Within the framework of Open Learning Communities, facilitators will work with local teams working in the community. Emphasis will be put on the identification of key situations, group process, and the development of alternatives in dealing with these situations. The basic approach here will be that of a snowballing multiplier system. We will open up an office in Angola, with two permanent staff members, that will serve as permanent liaison to the local teams. This is necessary because the political situation in Angola is quite unstable and the issue in itself so sensitive, the justified national mistrust against foreign institutions so high, that continuous contact and communication on the local level is necessary.

Networking is a highly difficult task always, and especially so when working in the area of trauma. Usually people are so immersed in their own traumatic reality, that although theoretically they all find networking a good idea, they never seem to find the time for it. Furthermore hope to develop a communicative structure that will permit participating institutions to mutually evaluate their work, thereby making it better and more apt to achieve the eternal search for funding. In the long run participants will thus obtain a mark of quality, comparable to the star system used by hotels. Using Internet, e-mail etc. start slowly, building up a trustworthy network from the beginning onwards, not because it is big - although would not mind that—but because it is good. The quantitative extension of public education in many countries during the 60's and 80's has undeniably brought about a certain amount of success, but at the same time led to a large-scale spreading of qualitative shortcomings, such as high dropout levels, rigid forms of teaching, the poor relation between some curricula and reality, and an examination system blown up out of all proportion.

In many countries the relationship between the educational system and the employment system is badly out of balance. The European myth fed by its privileged past, that the educational system would prepare qualified workers and the employment system subsequently offer the appropriate jobs, has turned out to be just as deceptive a belief as the hope, for example, which university graduates harbor in developing countries, that they will automatically receive jobs in the administration of large companies or in the civil service. In view of ever keener competition on the world market, education will increasingly only then mean better jobs when people learn to land on their own feet and to create jobs appropriate to world market conditions. Among other things this presupposes that professional pedagogues— hitherto used to an almost lifelong secure march through pedagogical institutions, and usually defensive by nature— also learn this lesson for themselves and act as appropriate role models. It is not enough here to limit oneself to advancing qualified employees, as if to imply that employer qualities such as innovative marketable ideas simply fall from heaven. Instead, it is necessary to promote an education for entrepreneurial behavior, an education for economy from below which begins at an early age and perceives entrepreneurial activity less as a personal peculiarity, and more as a basic qualification of the citoyen.

With this in mind, educational processes, subjects, and institutions can become counter-productive problems in themselves: the processes, as long as they adhere to a type of learning which barely accounts for the uncertainties of learning in real situations; the subject matter, as long as they ignore and suppress key problems of life under difficult conditions; the institutions, as long as they tend to represent the opposite of an entrepreneurial model in regard to structure and organization.The entire structure and program of colonial-style schools counteract the entrepreneurial potential of the majority of the population.

Learning is oriented towards real-life situations. 'Learning through life' means that learning processes should be encouraged in such real-life situations as much as possible. In this case, learning takes place not so much within parameters of a didactically arranged pretense of security, but rather in the openness of complex reality. It is an experience-oriented, inquisitive, experimenting, discovering type of learning in which theory and practice, reflection and action are all intimately interconnected with each other. Children have a right to learn material in context, to relate social with factual learning, and not be helplessly subjected to merely reduced and tailored forms of knowledge, but rather be encouraged to understand and explain the social contexts of meaningful activity. Children have a right to take part in designing situations in which they learn and act. They want to be challenged in their strengths, and not spoon-fed with pedagogical tranquilizers of occupational therapy. They have a right to be children and regarded as such (but not subjected to infantile treatment). Those who desire to help children on their way should do so with awareness of their individual development and chances of growth. To be empowered in real-life situations does not only mean possessing the necessary survival techniques, but also includes enhancing personal strength and the ability to entertain radical or different thoughts; it can also even mean the unhindered development of a craze or passion, the encouragement of wild play, or deep involvement in the arts, or expressions of feelings and bodily senses, movement and consciousness.

The context of normative behavior is to be explained over and over again, to counteract the split between 'moral' and 'technically instrumental competence' Educators and teachers do not behave as if giving orders from the command post, but rather as partners and impulse-givers: àsking, curious, sensitive, also learning. An open, situation-dependent planning replaces the usual rigid ritual. As with their children, the parents also take on a more central role in what is happening. To the extent that they can be present and want to be involved, they act as participants and active experts. Parents can offer a great variety of competent skills in key situations.

They help build bridges to the community. The situation approach reacts sensitively to minorities, opposes segregation, favors the integration of handicapped persons, invites interaction with other strangers, and values cultural variety in one world. The situation approach is always a form of community education, aims to open up pedagogical institutions and remove walls that block view. It counteracts the exclusion of childhood and youth from real-life activity, interprets learning as an integral part of community development, depends on the cooperation of professional pedagogues and competent members of the entire community, and taps learning venues within the community.

With the situation approach and the structural concept of the curriculum, a decisive step is attempted to make reality (to the extent it contains facts relevant to the issue) the immediate reference point for the development of educational processes and subject matter. This approach draws on sources of knowledge—academic as well as experience-based—and focuses them on real-life situations with their concomitant problem areas. The curriculum is hence organized according to key topics, problems, and situations and not according to subjects or departments. It does not follow the structure of any academic discipline, but rather instrumentalizes relevant methods and subject matters in order to explain and manage the situation.

Individualized Teaching

Some schools can be heard from far off: the teacher loudly speaks phrases, the whole class answers as one. Old-fashioned schools of this kind are to a large degree products of the colonial era, their classroom teaching methods still reflecting the spirit of the 19th and early 20th centuries. Teachers concentrate on covering each small portion of the fixed curriculum, and try not only to tame the horde of young lions in the class, but also bring them all to do the same thing at the same time. The style of mechanical learning employed is the most unsuitable conceivable for making sense of interrelationships, retaining what one has learned (even after the next exam), and applying knowledge gained. This is where a disastrous vicious circle of dequalification must be broken: insufficiently trained teachers behave like slaves to a detailed prescribed curriculum and force their students to reduce the great diversity of learning and experience down to the learning of textbooks by heart. When this mechanical system, which clearly contradicts the fundamental discoveries of modern learning theories, is then further underpinned by frequent tests and exams, one could even maintain that such a school is in the position of actually mutilating the qualifying potential of the next generation. Good test results achieved within this mechanism reveal very little about the ability to retain what one has learned, or creatively apply it in any given real situation.

Naturally there will still be some 'right' and 'wrong' answers. But in real-life situations there are often a number of different options which have to be compared and considered before making a decision. In any case, learning in connection with entrepreneurship also means learning how to think strategically while dealing with uncertainties, practicing to take calculated risks. There is a veritable arsenal of teaching methods and forms of pedagogical organization that serve these goals: teaching in small groups, learning and acting in projects, open or informal education, orienting the time frame to the task at hand and the current project, team teaching, mixed-aged groups and cross-generational learning. Classrooms can be transformed into learning workshops. At the same time, the limits of traditional school spaces will be dissolved: all the students will work with laptops and personal computers, and be able to communicate directly with teachers and other students electronically. Everyone will have access to libraries all over the world. In this interactive learning development, the concept of 'classroom' will surpass the traditional classroom.

Life in the Open Learning Community offers many chances of bringing a strong sense of self and an equally strong sense of community into a healthy relationship with each other, and preparing decisions by means of a democratic process of consensus building. Democracy does not exclude leadership—on the contrary, democracy depends on good leadership. Business enterprises also need strong leadership and the loyalty of their employees, but it is to the advantage of any business to keep up a meaningful dialog with its teams. The pupils will live separately according to sex, but not according to nationality or cultural heritage. Tolerance and respect is thus a highly valued virtue. Social responsibility is practiced, for instance, by work in some social or technical service such as a rescue service, the school fire department, technical relief organization, social services or environmental conservation service. The topography of the Open Learning Community contains a local network of facilities in Bali, and extends further into the wide world.

Learning for life situations also means learning in life situations. Hence fields of activity outside of the kindergarten will be integrated, so that the kindergarten truly becomes a part of the social network. The kindergarten teacher remains in close dialog with parents and families. The parents are not just onlookers, but rather personal authorities on the situations of their children. They take part in the kindergarten whenever they want to. In order to do this, it is important that the kindergarten be flexible with parents with regard to time and organization. Pupils of other nationalities need an international school. In order to make both alternatives a possible reality, a solution which allows for both kinds of schools is necessary. Each school has to fulfill its own requirements, but the two schools are more than that: they are to work closely together The school levels of the Indonesian School are divided into a Primary School for grades 1-6, a Junior High School for grades 7-9, and a

Senior High School for grades 10-12. Graduation is documented with the granting of an Indonesian Ijazah certificate. The school levels of the International School consist of a 4-year Primary School, a Secondary School for grades 5-10, and an International College for grades 11 and 12, which is completed with an International Baccalaureat. The boundaries between the school grades will not have very much particular importance in daily practice, but rather only represent a general demarcation. Actually the main thing is that pupils in grades 5-12 grow up together and are encouraged and challenged according to their general age level. As of the fifth school year, children can be accepted to the Boarding School. This applies to Indonesian children as well as those of other nationalities. Most likely a small portion of these boarding school students will attend the national school; the majority will attend the international school.

Today we would speak of 'holistic' and 'learning by experience', perhaps also of learning by doing. - Schools are not only there to instruct the heads, but just as much to educate and develop the senses, feelings, physical health, manual dexterity. The senses, feelings, body and hands also have to be able to have experiences which encourage and promote them and thus help 'educate' the person as a human being." Tourism is frequently staged far away from the truly interesting situations and opportunities of the country. Tourism can contribute to the destruction of regional cultures. However, that properly handled tourism can support and promote regional cultures and contribute to their development, that an individualized, authentic tourism can act as culturally enriching and serve ethnic understanding, that it can provide great pleasure as well as be the economically better concept to make intelligent friends and partners out of the previous opposing "dumb tourist" and broad mass of "natives".

On the one hand the Center is a program which brings guests together with culturally, politically, and economically leading families of the local and regional area in Bali, and allows them topersonally enjoy their hospitality. On the other hand it provides guests who are looking for social and cultural contrasts with expeditions and projects concerning various island realities. All the projects have a playful and enjoyable character. The 'scholarly concept' of the Center is founded on elements of action research, discovery learning, and sensual experience. It does not assume expert knowledge, but only a healthy common sense, curiosity, and the joy of discovery. One of its essential aspects is that native people and guests get to know each other, and that guests make contacts among each other as well. The guests can document the results of these activities themselves if they so desire. A guest library will be set up. so that the progress of the various projects can be followed and reconstructed for new guests who join in later, or for those guests who might return and who want to check up on what has been done in their absence. The activities will be reported on locally and internationally: on the local level, the native people experience the results of the projects.

The students act as trace-seekers, the developer of paths into an interesting reality. They take care of the guests during their research activities and learn by direct participation. In doing so they also learn how to work with the guests in an articulate, culturally competent and imaginative manner. The curriculum of this Center deals with general knowledge concerning tourism and management, as well as specific historical, religious, cultural, artistic, architectural, geographical, biological, and ecological knowledge of Bali. A cultural authentic tourism as practiced here in a small-scale model also makes good sense. In US, the majority of the pupils will originate from places far away from Bali. For their parents this means that visiting their children involves a great deal of travel. In order to make their stay on the island as pleasant as possible, on the one hand parents are invited to participate in activities of the school when and as they please, and on the other hand they are to be made to feel as comfortable as possible as guests.

Case Methodology On-line

The collision of technology and case methodology was inevitable. The combination of technology and case-based instruction gave birth to new applications of case methodology in teacher and principal preparation programs, for example video-cases, computer-based simulations, virtual case competitions on the World Wide Web, cases presented as CD-ROM and laser disks, and electronic meeting systems. The technological formats of case analysis can be written, spoken, or based in hypermedia utilizing the Internet or World Wide Web. Unlike the traditional classroom discussion of cases, electronic meeting systems (EMS) allow for constant ongoing dialogue between participants. Moreover, electronic brainstorming produces significantly more fresh ideas than traditional classroom analysis of cases. EMS also allows more people to interact without interruption and to input ideas simultaneously.

Opportunity for the participation of all group members is also enhanced in computer-mediated case discussions. On-line case discussion in the York University PQP resonates with the need to decrease the gap between classroom instruction and practice and to enhance students' ability to make good decisions that are at the core of school leadership. Feedback plays an important role in the learning process: as people receive information about the results of their actions, they are able to correct themselves progressively until they achieve the intended results. Although one face-to-face meeting of the on-line groups is scheduled during the course, candidates may never meet their on-line mentor or other members of their on-line group. Group cohesion is developed through a combination of required participation, the skill of the on-line mentor, and the ongoing involvement of the participants. Case methodology has changed in recent years from the method of instruction based on face-to-face discussion of oral cases/narratives confined to the classroom space to computer-mediated asynchronous discussion of on-line cases in virtual classrooms/cyber-classrooms. Narratives in cyberspace, rather than being a part of an oral discourse, entail new communicative styles and ways of engagement with texts/cases on the part of the learners. In theorizing of learning, claims have been made that learn from the other's response to what convey. Thus, learning the art of school leadership through on-line narratives necessitates the learners to put their responses out there and to find out what comes back.

According to the National Center for Education Statistics, between fall 1995 and 1997-98, the percentage of higher education institutions offering distance learning courses increased by one-third, and the number of course offerings and enrollments approximately doubled. But although many institutions have delivered distance learning via mail, radio, or television for years, this growth is not in those media. Rather, it is distance learning via the Internet that is booming. Among all higher-education institutions offering any distance learning, the percentage of institutions using asynchronous Internet-based technologies nearly tripled, from 22% in 1995 to 60% in 1997-1998. More recent data from Market Data Retrieval (MDR) confirm the trend. MDR relates that, as of the 1999-2000 academic year, 34% of two- and four-year colleges offered accredited degree programs via computer, up from 15% the year before. As of 2000, U.S. institutions reportedly offered more than 6,000 accredited courses on the Web and, by 2002, over 2 million students will be enrolled, a tripling of the 1998 enrollment. At the same time, Internet-based distance learning is finding its way into high school. The growth of Internet-based distance learning will have a significant impact upon traditional education. For one, it may threaten the existence of established institutions. Many in the private sector see education as a huge industry that produces mediocre results for a high cost. If the private sector can leverage new technologies, like distance learning, to deliver greater value, the institutions that dominate education today will not be the leaders tomorrow. The rapid growth of for-profit education companies, and the seemingly endless creation of well-capitalized new ones, suggests that a serious challenge to the existing order is well underway. The gravity of the threat is evident in how non-profits have responded. A second reason that the growth of Internet-based distance learning will influence traditional education is that regardless of its impact on nonprofit institutions, the distance learning industry will produce sophisticated software that everyone can use, in school and out.

The considerable potential of online learning—local or distance—is reflected in a report to the President and Congress of the bipartisan Web-Based Education Commission. The question is no longer if the Internet can be used to transform learning in new and powerful ways. The Commission has found that it can. Nor is the question should we invest the time, the energy, and the money necessary to fulfill its promise in defining and shaping new learning opportunity. As online learning becomes more widespread, the substance and format of assessment will need to keep pace. So, as students do more and more of their learning using technology tools, asking them to express that learning in a medium different from the one they typically work in will become increasingly untenable, especially where working with the medium is part of the skill being tested. These changes in learning methodology offer exciting possibilities for assessment innovation. On site or off, an obvious result of delivering courses via the Internet is the potential for embedding assessment, perhaps almost seamlessly, in instruction. Since students respond to instructional exercises electronically, their responses can be recorded, leaving a continuous learning trace. Depending upon how the course and the assessment are designed, this information could conceivably support a sophisticated model of student proficiencies. That model might be useful both for dynamically deciding what instruction to present next and for making more global judgments about what the student knows and can do at any given point. In addition to assessment embedded in Internet-delivered courses, one can imagine Internet-delivered-assessment embedded in traditional classroom activity.

Such assessment might take the form of periodically delivered exercises that both teach and test. In this scenario, the exercises would be standardized and performance might serve, depending upon the level of aggregation, to indicate individual, classroom, school, district, state, or national achievement. Thus, these exercises could serve summative as well as formative purposes and be useful to individuals as well as institutions. A continuing concern with such reinvention visions is whether schools (and students) are ready technologically and, in particular, what to do about technology differences across social groups. The National Center for Education Statistics (NCES) reports that as of September 1999, around 95% of schools were connected to the Internet, up from 35% in 1994.

Schools in all categories, (i.e., by grade level, poverty concentration, and metropolitan status), were equally likely to have Internet access. Further, most schools had dedicated lines: only 14% were using dial-up modem, a slower and less reliable access method. Clearly many of these schools could have only a single connected machine and that machine could be the one sitting on the principal's desk. The government's e-rate program has been giving public schools and libraries discounts of up to 90% on phone service, Internet hook-ups, and wiring for several years. In total, the program has committed 3.65 billion dollars to over 50,000 institutions, helping connect more than one million public school classrooms. In addition, 70% of the program's last round of funding went to schools in the lowest income areas. However, even with these very significant efforts, there continue to be equity issues. As of September 1999, in high poverty schools, the ratio of students to Internet computers was 16 to 1. Certainly, with few exceptions, it would be impossible to deliver large-scale assessment via the Internet today. But the trend is clear: the infrastructure is quickly falling into place for Internet delivery of assessment to schools, perhaps first in survey programs like NAEP that require only a small participant sample from each school, but eventually for inclusive assessments delivered directly to the desktop.

Sustaining technologies enhance the performance of established products in ways that mainstream customers have traditionally valued. Historically, most technological advances in any given industry have been sustaining ones. Occasionally, disruptive technologies emerge. Companies introduce these technologies hoping their features will provide competitive edge. However, these features characteristically overshoot the market, giving customers more than they need or are willing to pay for. Thus, disruptive technologies result in worse product performance, at least in the near-term, on key dimensions in a company's established markets. Interestingly, a few fringe customers typically find a disruptive technology's new features attractive. In these niche markets, such technology may thrive. If and when it advances to the level and nature of performance demanded in the mainstream market, the new technology can invade it, rapidly knocking out the traditional technology and its dependent practitioners.

CBT has many of the characteristics of a disruptive technology. Established testing organizations are applying it in their mainstream markets, most notably postsecondary admissions. This innovation was introduced, in good part, to provide competitive edge through features like the ability to take a test at one's convenience and to get score reports immediately. As it turned out, these features overshot the market. At least initially, registrations for continuously-offered computer-based admissions tests mirrored those for fixed-date administrations, suggesting that scheduling convenience was not a highly valued feature in the market of the time. Moreover, examinees were dissatisfied with losing some of the features of paper exams, including the ability to proceed through the test nonlinearly, the option to review the scoring of items actually taken, and the low cost. Although it encountered difficulty in the mainstream admissions testing market, CBT found more rapid acceptance in the niches.

One example is information technology (IT) certification, which individuals pursue to document their competence in some computer-related proficiency. In 1999, over three million examinations in 25 languages were administered in this market. Most of these tests were delivered on computer and most were offered on a continuous basis. Let's start by asking what features a testing product must have to succeed in this niche. First, it must be continuously offered because these test candidates build technology skill on their own schedules—at home or on the job, very often through books or online learning. These individuals want to test when they are ready, not when the testing companies are. Second, such a test must generally be offered on computer since technology use is the essence of the certification. Security is not as critical as in admissions testing, so large item pools are not needed, reducing production cost. Lower security is tolerable because if an individual appears on the job with a dishonestly obtained credential but without the required skill, he or she will not last. Finally, test volume is self-replicating: there are many repeat test takers because information technology changes rapidly, so skills must be updated constantly.

From an innovation perspective, then, IT certification may be one context in which the CBT of today can flourish and develop to better meet the needs of other assessment markets. Industry leaders often fail precisely because they attempt to introduce disruptive technologies into major markets before it's time. The Industry leaders do not pursue those opportunities to refine the technology. Instead, they give up, having run out of resources or credibility. Making a disruptive technology work requires iteration and iteration means failure. Because they risk neither large resources nor reputations in the mainstream market, it is the fringe players who can fail early, often, and inexpensively enough to eventually challenge and overtake the industry leaders.

Electronic Textbooks

Developing adaptive electronic textbooks on WWW based on the ideas from the areas of Intelligent Tutoring Systems and Adaptive Hypermedia. Adaptive textbooks use knowledge about its domain and about its users. The domain model serves as a basis for structuring the content of an adaptive ET. There are two parts in an adaptive ET: a glossary and a textbook. Both these parts are based on the domain model. The student model is used by an adaptive ET to adapt its behaviour to each particular user. The key to adaptivity in an adaptive ET are the domain model and the user model. The simplest form of domain model is just a set of domain concepts. By concepts mean elemntary pieces of knowledge for the given domain. Depending on the domain and the application area, concepts can represent bigger or smaller pieces of domain knowledge. A more advanced form of the domain model is a network with nodes corresponding to domain concepts and with links reflecting several kinds of relationships between concepts. This network represents the structure of the domain covered by a hypermedia system. The domain model provides a structure for representation of the user's knowledge of the subject. For each domain model concept, an individual user's knowledge model stores some value which is an estimation of the user knowledge level of this concept.

The glossary is the central part of the ET. The glossary is considered as a visualized (and externalized) domain network. Each node of the domain network is represented by a node of the hyperspace, while the links between domain network nodes constitute main paths between hyperspace nodes. The structure of the glossary resembles the pedagogical structure of the domain knowledge and, vise versa, each glossary entry corresponds to one of the domain concepts. The links between domain model concepts constitute navigation paths between glossary entries. Thus, the structure of the manual resembles the pedagogic structure of the domain knowledge. In addition to providing a description of a concept, each glossary entry provides links to all book sections which introduce the concept. It means that the glossary integrates traditional features of an index and a glossary. A textbook is hierarchically structured into units of different level: chapters, sections, and subsections. To make the textbook 'more intelligent' and to connect it to the glossary, to let the system know what each unit of the textbook is about. It is done by indexing of textbook units with domain model concepts. For each unit, a list of concepts related with this unit is provided. For each involved concept, the spectrum of the unit can represents also the role of the concept in the unit. Currently support two roles: each concept can be either a outcome concept or a prerequisite concept.

A concept is included in the spectrum as a outcome concept if some part of this page presents the piece of knowledge designated by the concept. A concept is included in the spectrum as a prerequisite concept if a user has to know this concept to understand the content of the page. Indexing is a relatively simple but powerful mechanism, because it provides the system with knowledge about the content of its pages: the system knows which concepts are presented on each page and which concepts have to be learned before starting to learn each page. It opens the way for several adaptation techniques presented in the next subsection. The knowledge about the domain and about the textbook content is used to serve a well-structured hyperspace. The system supports sequential and hierachical links between section. It generates the table of content where all entries are clickable links. In addition, it generates links between the glossary and the textbook. Links are provided from each textbook unit to corresponding glossary pages for each involved concept.

On the other hand, from each glossary page describing a concept the system provides links to all textbook units which can be used to learn this concept. These links are not stored in an external format but generated on-the-fly by a special module which takes into account the user's current state of knowledge represented by the user's model. This approach is not only reducing page design time but also provides room for adaptation. Many more opportunities for browsing the course materials than traditional on-line textbooks. The negative side of it is that there is a higher risk for the user to get lost in this complex hyperspace. To support the user navigating through the course, the system uses adaptive annotation, an adaptive hypermedia technique. Adaptive annotation means that the system uses visual cues (icons, fonts, colors) to show the type and the educational state of each link. Using the user model, the system can distinguish several educational states for each page of material: the content of the page can be known to the user, ready to be learned, or not ready to be learned (the latter example means that some prerequisite knowledge is not yet learned).

The icon and the font of each link presented to the user are computed dynamically from the individual user model. They always inform the user about the type and the educational state of the node behind the link. Red means not ready to be learned, green means ready and recommended, and white means no new information. A checkmark is added for already visited sections. The system knowledge about the course material comprises knowledge about what the prerequisite concepts are for any unit of the textbook. Often, when users have problems with understanding some explanation or example or solving a problem, the reason is that some prerequisite material is not understood well. In that case they can request prerequisite-based help (using a special button) and, as an answer to help request, the system generate a list of links to all sections which present some information about background concepts of the current section. This list is adaptively sorted according to the user's knowledge represented in the user model: more 'helpful' sections are listed first. Here 'helpful' means how informative the section is to learn about the background concepts. For example, the section which presents information about an unknown background concept is more informative then a section presenting information about a known concept. The section which presents information about two unknown background concepts is more informative then a section presenting information about one concept.

Hypermedia and WWW

The most obvious way to bring ITS to WWW is to port some existing ITS technologies to WWW. The most relevant technique for that is intelligent knowledge sequencing and problem sequencing. Intelligent knowledge sequencing implies adaptive selection of the next topic to be learned using the student model and the knowledge about the learning material. Intelligent problem sequencing in the narrow sense implies choosing or generating the next problem for the student to solve, which should be most relevant to his level of knowledge and skills. In a broader sense it implies adaptive sequencing of all kinds of teaching operations—examples, tests, problems, questions, etc. In a hypermedia systems intelligent knowledge sequencing is usually considered as intelligent sequencing of hypermedia pages or hypernodes. In addition to regular (prescribed) hypermedia buttons or active fields the student is provided with dynamic 'intelligent button' called 'next' or 'teach-me' which activates knowledge sequencing mechanism. This button brings the student to the hypernode, which is most relevant to him from system's point of view. Intelligent problem sequencing is usually implemented by the same way—the student is provided with a dynamic button which activates sequencing mechanism. As a result the student is presented with the most relevant problem to solve for the currently studied topic or for the course in general. Implementation of intelligent sequencing within hypermedia framework brings new quality by combining student-directed and guided learning. It provides some solution for 'getting lost' problem of hypermedia: the learner who can hardly find his own way in hyperspace can now use system guided navigation. At the same time it provides some benefits over traditional 'directed' ITS style of teaching: the students who are not satisfied with system-directed sequencing can use hypermedia style of browsing the learning material.

Integration of ITS and WWW hypermedia technologies provides a new quality in one more sense: it opens the way to some new intelligent techniques, which are based on both ITS and hypermedia paradigms and which are new in the ITS domain. Adaptive hypermedia is a good example of such a technique. As in general hypermedia system, the educational process here is driven by the student. The difference is that adaptive hypermedia systems can use the student model and some other knowledge typical to ITS to adapt its work to the given student. In particular, it can be used to guide the student implicitly. Adaptive hypermedia systems bridge the gap between computer-driven tutoring systems and student-driven educational environments. They combines free browsing with personalization and can support not just two ends (as classic ITS and hypermedia), but all the continuum of learning modes between pure system-controlled and student-controlled. What can be adapted in adaptive hypermedia are the content of a hypermedia page and the links from a page to related pages.

We distinguish these two techniques of adaptation and call the first technique adaptive presentation (or content-level adaptation) and the second technique adaptive navigation support (or link-level adaptation). Adaptive presentation is the most popular and the most studied way of hypermedia adaptation. With adaptive presentation the content of a hypermedia page is generated or assembled from pieces according to the user's class and knowledge state. Generally, qualified users receive more detailed and deep information, while novices receive more additional explanation. Two popular application areas for adaptive presentation are adaptive hypermedia-based help in knowledge-based systems and on-line documentation systems. By adaptive navigation support mean all the ways to play with visible links which can support hyperspace navigation. In current systems, three kinds of adaptive navigation support have been suggested and implemented: hiding a part of links, adaptive ordering of visible links, and adaptive annotation of visible links. Hiding of a part of visible links was used in. ated nodes according to user knowledge and goals.

5

Challenges of Technology and Teachers

Today many teachers have difficulties developing strategies to manage their classrooms effectively - strategies that enable them to concentrate on supporting students rather than discipline. Although educational institutions spoke about the importance of enabling educators to bring a more diagnostic perspective to their teaching, this approach is not so effectively supported or sustained once teachers enter the classroom.

Supporting new teachers in their first few years of classroom practice is a widely recognized problem for both universities and schools. Where new teachers are in steady communication with either university faculty or experienced master teachers in their schools, are an increasingly common way to bridge the gap between the pedagogical ideas encountered in teacher education courses and the reality of K-12 practice. There are many ways to name the problem for new teachers. They are suddenly confronted with a classroom full of children whose needs are real, immediate, and varied. Issues of classroom management are among the first to become apparent even if there is a shared curriculum and a full supply of resources. Eventually, assessment issues loom for new teachers. They often lack the experience to recognize appropriate indicators of progress or of misconceptions that have impeded a student's understanding (or ability to demonstrate that understanding).

Time—how to manage it, how to use it well, how to find more of it both for preparation and for reflection about practice—is the single most dramatic issue for most new teachers—and perhaps for all teachers. University or school-based mentors can provide a supportive shoulder, can give good advice and useful ideas for practice, but they cannot supervise closely. They cannot be there as new teachers attempt to organize their students' work or diagnose their progress on a regular basis. Recent progress in the development of new wireless handheld technology provides a potential opportunity for a richer and more concrete communication between mentors and new teachers. These new small, flexible, and easy-to-use computational devices permit a new kind of sharing of concrete, specific information about student work that can form the basis for more immediately useful conversations among educators about their daily practice.

Collaborated with a technology company, Wireless Generation, interested in developing new tools for teachers and a suburban school district, Mamaroneck, New York, which had the human and technological infrastructure to support such experimentation. This experiment with new teachers. Instead, worked with experienced teachers in order to identify potential uses of the technology that fit realistically into daily classroom practice. It is assumption that new teachers might eventually learn to use these devices during their training and then continue to use them both to organize their teaching and to communicate with their mentors during the early years of their practice. First, however, had to investigate what makes sense with experienced teachers who could help us design appropriate programs. In the course of collaborating with teachers and administrators in the district, decided on two applications that addressed aspects of two major problems for new teachers: classroom management and diagnostic assessment.

Classroom Management

Special education teachers about classroom management because the district has an inclusion policy and special education teachers follow their students to regular classrooms and help them organize their work in a way that is appropriate to the students' developmental level. Each teacher follows a group of students to different classrooms, which presents a serious organizational challenge. This challenge is not identical to the one faced by new teachers in regular classrooms. It is, however, a new way of working for all of the special education teachers and intended to investigate if the use of the handheld technology could support new ways of working and save teachers time. Teachers ended up using not special software, but the kinds of productivity tools built into the Palm Organizer to keep track of their students' assignments. The ability to beam customized assignments to their students and have students beam back their checklists made it much easier for teachers to keep track of their students' work.

The district uses a 'balanced reading' approach in elementary school, which includes the keeping of 'running records.' In short, this technique involves regular one-to-one sessions during which a teacher keeps track of every word read by an individual student from a set of books that have been categorized according to established reading levels. As the student reads, the teacher uses a form to monitor how the child is deciphering the text. Each incorrect word is noted and the nature of the misreading is charted according to a pre-determined code. Based on this diagnostic assessment, teachers then determine whether the child is ready to read a book on a higher level.

Special software on the Palm Organizer makes these tasks much easier to accomplish and also summarizes and graphs each student's reading performance, allowing for easy comparisons so teachers can see at a glance how children are progressing. Teachers can also share that information instantly with other teachers, administrators, and potentially with parents. The teachers are observed found the running-record-keeping software easy to use and eagerly anticipate the next version, which will summarize achievement.

In US, the Palm Pilot project in Hommocks Middle School (HMS) took place in the special education department, which has 175 students and teachers. Every special education teacher has a team of students who participate in the general education classes (inclusion students). Until this academic year students with special learning needs 1 attended reinforcement groups with a special education teacher. This year the school started a new inclusion model. Instead of working with reinforcement groups, the special education teachers attended the general education classrooms in order to support their team of students. The special education staff at HMS felt the experiment was very successful. In a recent survey they found that the general education students assume that the support teachers are there to support all the students, not only those with special learning needs.

In the Palm inclusion project, handheld computers were viewed primarily as organizational tools. The project aimed to help students master organizational skills, keep track of their assignments, and make sure they knew what to bring to school. Since special education students have organizational problems, they find these skills difficult to master. They tend to forget what they have to do, to leave their assignments at home, to do half of their work, etc.

Currently, students copy their homework assignments off the blackboard to a planner, and special education students who have difficulty with transcription or word order often copy down the wrong assignment. With Palm Pilots, teachers could beam assignments directly to students' calendars and "To Do" lists.

Teachers could help students organize their work by breaking assignments down into short-term intermediary deadlines to meet longer-term goals. Parents of students with special needs are often very involved in helping their child organize work.

One goal of the project was to help students become more autonomous by organizing and taking responsibility for their own learning. The students in this rsult were at an age when most children are beginning to resent adult involvement but still need a good deal of steady support, a combination that is particularly true for students with learning disabilities. For these students, Palm Pilots had the additional advantage of being non-stigmatizing, even 'cool.'

Teachers hoped that use of the technology would enable them to be more aware of the work progress of their special education students. They also hoped that technology-supported communication with each other would facilitate sharing information about their students, which is particularly important when students rotate among classes and work with more than one teacher.

Students quickly mastered writing their homework assignments on their Palms. Occasionally they beamed assignments to each other. For the most part, it was unnecessary for teachers to beam assignments to students. The teachers developed their own ways of using the Palms. One teacher wrote the assignments on her desktop, hot-synched them to her Palm, and beamed them to all of her students daily. Another teacher checked her students' Palms daily to make sure they had all their assignments written down, and in rare cases beamed them what they were missing.

One teacher posted the assignments daily on her website. Initially, the project aimed to use the Palm as an organizer and as a communication tool between teachers and students in order to make sure students recorded all of their assignments. This turned out to be unnecessary in most cases, since students mastered the device much more quickly and were more comfortable with it than their teachers so that the teachers' intervention was not required. Students, on the other hand, beamed each other notes and assignments when they were missing something.

Based on the preliminary findings of this formative, the classroom management uses of technology have potential for preservice education. In this case, teachers used the technology to keep track of what their learning disabled students were doing in inclusive classrooms. Both teachers and students used the handheld computers to organize work. Even though handheld organizers are not yet considered essential in schools, the enormous growth of these tools in the business community is bound to have the usual ripple effect in the educational community. It is not entirely unrealistic to expect that both teachers and students will soon consider an electronic organizer a normal part of school equipment, especially as the price of such devices continues to drop.

Attendance, assignments, assessments, and other forms of record keeping can be done more efficiently with small, flexible, genuinely portable devices. Cutting down on paperwork in this way by making record keeping easier and by permitting instant sharing of such records with school administrators may have a positive effect on how new teachers use their time. The ability to share those records with mentors and administrators may alert them to developing problems that require extra attention and support.

The district uses a 'balanced reading' approach in its elementary schools that includes the keeping of 'running records.' In short, this technique involves regular one-to-one session during which a teacher keeps track of every word read by an individual student from a set of books that have been categorized according to established reading levels. As the student reads, the teacher uses a form (based on the Reading Recovery model prevalent in many schools) to monitor how the child is deciphering the text. Each incorrect word is noted and the nature of the misreading is charted according to a pre-determined code. Based on this diagnostic assessment, teachers then determine whether the child is ready to read a book on a higher level. Wireless Generation, Inc. developed a software application for the Palm Pilot to support this running record process. The software permits teachers to keep their records on their Palms rather than on paper.

The software accepts handwritten input and summarizes and graphs each student's reading performance, allowing for easy comparisons so that teachers can see at a glance how children are progressing. The technology allows teachers to share that information instantly with other teachers through infrared beaming and with administrators and potentially with parents, through synching their handheld computers with a desktop computer and sending the information to a shared website.

The district focuses considerable effort on its early literacy program. They are persuaded that a balanced approach, combining techniques developed by the Reading Recovery process with those of other early literacy programs, best serves their community. They were hoping that the handheld computer version of the running records technique would facilitate and standardize the recording process.

Administrators focused on the promise of making everyone's records more standardized and more easily available as well as on making more informed choices about instructional strategies in conversations between individual teachers and reading consultants. Teachers focused on the promise of saving time by making the recording easier to conduct, save, analyze, and share.

The emphasis in the research was on gathering enough information about how the process being supported by technology works in real classrooms to make it possible for Wireless Generation to develop a small, powerful, flexible application that does exactly what teachers need. Since the process was not being invented by the participating teachers, there were many sources of information in addition to classroom observations and interviews with teachers and administrators, including the Reading Recovery movement literature and specialized conferences on early literacy.

Wireless Generation staff attended conferences and read the background literature to make sure they understood the theory underlying the method as well as the practice. In practice, individual teachers take records in different ways and interpret the results of their record keeping differently. Wireless Generation and CCT staff observed them, interviewed them, and went through an iterative process of showing them templates that reflect their practice.

In February, seven participating K-2 teachers used their Palms with a beta version of the running record application to conduct their student recordings. All seven successfully conducted several recordings. When the original software was updated at the end of the month, their original recordings were inadvertently lost. This discouraged them from continuing to use the application until a reliable synching and backup system was devised. The web-based database, which will eventually store the data from individual recordings, is still under development at this time.

The teachers are observed found the running-record-keeping software easy to use and eagerly anticipate the next version, which will summarize achievement. Meanwhile, however, they continue to make use of their Palms to organize their own work. Their personal uses range from storing contact information about their students in the address book, to writing notes, to using the calendar to schedule meetings and the 'To Do' list to keep track of paperwork that must be done.

The software was still under development throughout this project and continues to be as of this writing. As a result, these observations are very preliminary, but they allow us to speculate about the potential of handheld technology for teacher preparation.

1. The single most powerful affordance of this flexible, highly portable technology is its ability to make certain aspects of teachers' thinking visible through easy and instant sharing.

2. Keeping track of student performance digitally saves time. It makes the recording process easier and, since the information is already in digital form, no additional time is required to make it available for sharing.

3. The portability of the handheld devices and the ability to enter information easily through simple clicks and handwritten notes make it possible to collect information about student performance easily, both during planned occasions and spontaneously as opportunities arise.

4. The ability to keep track of student performance this way provides a kind of process recording that can be shared with other teachers and university faculty and

form the basis for far more concretely informed conversations between new teachers and their mentors.

5. It enables mentors to observe how teachers-in-training are learning to use the assessment tools at their disposal (in this case running reading records) and to adjust their professional development efforts accordingly.
6. Once a new teacher has mastered the recording process, the ease with which the process recordings can be shared provides mentors with an opportunity to observe what the students of new teachers are accomplishing.
7. The dual opportunity to assess the observation and recording skills of the new teachers, and the learning progress of their students, promises to be highly useful when teachers-in-training are sent out to do their student-teaching in diverse settings because it allows university faculty to augment site visits with a flow of process information, easily available because already in digital form.
8. The software itself provides tools for reflection. The ability to view student progress in charts and graphs and to compare students encourages reflection about student performance.
9. The software encourages reflection about teaching strategies by providing summaries, comparisons, and reminders about when students might be ready to move to a new level of challenge.
10. The portability of the information means that reflection about student performance and progress can take place at different times, when it is most

convenient for the teacher. With the use of this new technology, teachers no longer have to go to the information they need in order to reflect; instead, the information can come with them wherever they go.

Other educational software packages help clarify student performance, but until the appearance of handheld computers, they have always required being near a desktop computer to take advantage of them. The school day is so full for most teachers, and particularly so for new teachers, that expecting them to spend a portion of their time in front of a computer terminal somewhere—even if at their desk—reflecting on student progress, is unrealistic and unreasonable. What makes this portable technology genuinely interesting is not only that it can save a teacher time, but that the time it saves is more likely to be filled with reflection about the meaning of the collected data because the software itself supports and facilitates such reflection. Expect that the conversations with mentors or university faculty can be focused more on reflection and interpretation than on reporting of information because the software's record keeping and comparison functions allow mentors to consider information about student performance ahead of time.

Handheld technologies are likely to prove very useful in supporting new teachers as they leave universities and encounter the increasingly complex challenge of being a teacher held accountable for preparing students for full citizenship in the information age. These technologies can help build a digital bridge over the gap between teacher preparation and entering the profession. There are two distinctly different uses of the technology: as a tool for organizing the educational work-flow for teachers and students, and as a diagnostic assessment tool. There are many other potential uses, including a vast set of possible instructional uses, from data-gathering expeditions to analytic tools and simulations, to sharing notes, information, or ideas. Portability, genuinely ubiquitous access, is the single most powerful feature of these new devices. Portability includes the access to wireless networks and infrared beaming among wireless devices. Without the capacity to share information stored on a device, these computers would still have enormous value for education, but the ability to share information so easily makes them particularly flexible and powerful. The small size and light weight of these devices makes ubiquitous access a reality. Teachers (and students) really can carry them around everywhere. The input accepted by these devices makes ubiquitous access possible because they:

— Recognize handwriting reasonably well (and will continue to improve)

— Digitize hand-drawn images as well as accept digital photos

Have built-in touch screens which allow input with almost any pointer, including a finger

— Have a built-in soft keyboard which allows more standardized data entry

— Have a number of useful peripherals, including good, full-size, but lightweight and highly portable keyboards for extensive writing and modem cards for telecommunication.

These features make it possible to keep track of all kinds of information spontaneously and systematically. Teachers and students can jot down an impression in a few words or make a quick drawing and annotate it (they can even take a quick digital snapshot of a work in progress). All of these notes are permanently stored and easily retrievable for analysis and sharing. Making the 'stuff' of observed experience more easily available supports reflection. It also provides the means of illustrating a student's record of achievement with examples of real work, teachers' reflections, as well as demographic data and test results, thus supporting a more holistic form of record keeping.

The running records application is an example of how this technology can be used to support more individualized assessment. In particular, the technology supports a more diagnostic approach to assessment because the built-in capacity to instantly compare student performance over time and with other students puts any single assessment into an appropriate and meaningful context. Running records is an early literacy assessment program. Undoubtedly, other, comparable uses for small, flexible applications will be developed that scaffold the process for new teachers and facilitate recording and sharing among all users of a technique. In the area of preservice education, then, the promise of handheld technology is most likely to lie in helping to:

— Organize a new teacher's work

— Facilitate communication between teachers and students

— Facilitate information sharing between teachers and mentors

— Provide primary material for systematic analysis and reflection

Scaffold particular instructional or assessment techniques through the use of customized recording templates.

Further development will be needed to determine other, perhaps more instructional, uses of these devices. Meanwhile, however, they can be used effectively both 'as is,' by helping to organize a new (and usually overwhelmed) teacher's work, and with customized, specific applications, to support and scaffold the use of particular instructional and assessment techniques.

Challenges of Technology Use in Education

A September 2002, the review of the US Center for Education Statistics highlighted the rapid pace of change in schools as a result of this massive infusion of capital. The percentage of schools connected to the Internet increased from 35 percent in 1994 to 99 percent in 2001. The student to Internet connected computer ratio has improved dramatically in an even shorter time frame, going from 12 students per computer in 1998 to 5 to 1 in 2001. Likewise, there has been a significant rise in teachers using computers and networks for planning and instruction. *A Nation Online*, released in early 2002 by the U.S. Department of Commerce, showed that American children who lack access to computers and the Internet at home are relying on wired schools and libraries for access. For example, thanks to these public access facilities, nearly 90 percent of all school-aged children (aged 5-17) use computers and 59 percent used the Internet-making American children the most connected in the world. Just over 80 percent of children (aged 10-17) in the lowest income category were using computers at school, little different from the 89 percent of children from households in the highest income category. Hispanic and Black children, who have much lower computer use rates at home, approach the overall computer use rates of Whites and Asian American/ Pacific Islander children largely because of public access:

> 84 percent for Hispanic children, 89 percent for Black children, 94 percent for Asian/Pacific Islander children, and 95 percent for White children. However, a far higher percentage of Hispanic (39 percent) and Black (45 percent) children rely solely on public access facilities to use computers than White children (15 percent).

Despite this good news, students say more needs to be done to ensure get a full return on the nation's IT investment in schools. According to a 2002 Pew Internet and American Life, The Digital Disconnect:

> The widening gap between Internet-savvy students and their schools, students said it was imperative to connect classrooms and not just schools, ensure that all students master computer literacy skills, and train teachers to create assignments that take advantage of Internet resources they found on their own. Similarly, technology coordinators indicated in a National School Boards Foundation results, that schools are not taking full advantage of technology as a tool to improve teaching and learning. It is not enough to install computers and wire classrooms for Internet access, although there is still plenty of work to do in this regard. Today, the focus needs to expand to how schools are using technology.

A focus on effective classroom use is hampered by the current economic climate and the changing role of the federal government related to educational technology. These changes have resulted in school IT investments coming under greater scrutiny than ever—with a heightened focus on measurable results. The years 2001 and 2002 saw the stock market tumble and with it state, local and federal budget revenue. It is possible that state and local administrators may use the new transfer authority of the No Child Left Behind Act (NCLB) and begin to pull back from fully implementing and funding edtech programmes, believing them to be ineffective or arguing that the funding would be better spent elsewhere.

Most recently, in January 2002, published in Great Expectations: Leveraging America's Investment in Education Technology, an outline of the findings from an 18-month. The state of educational technology and outlined needed steps to ensure that national edtech investments were maximized. These included recommendations for improvements to the E-Rate (i.e. the education rate, or the Federal Communications Commission's $2.25 billion a year in telecommunication's discounts to schools and libraries), new strategies and models for assessing students' technology-based work, and a state and local framework for assessing and improving edtech implementation.

The team from the Center for Children and Technology provides an overview of their sustainability framework, using as a context their field work in various U.S. cities and review of the relevant literature. The particular challenges that face schools in Indian Country as they seek to ensure digital opportunities for all their students. From work on programme contend that it is imperative for schools to leverage the large edtech investments they have made to date, to maintain the infrastructure they have in place and be strategic about upgrading and supporting networks in the future. If local schools do not develop the talents of staff, if they do not rethink how edtech can be more effective in fulfilling their core missions and, if they do not provide technical support and incentives for trained professionals to stay, then this first wave of edtech investments will have been badly made. Even as the focuses on improvements in how schools use and maintain their instructional technology infrastructure, a pressing and related issue is home access for all students.

The students interviewed in the Pew studies expressed a serious concern about the digital divide, or the lack of home access to computers and the Internet of their less fortunate peers. As in other calculations, the tech-savvy students who were surveyed indicated that most of their computer work and learning took place at home. These students realized their less fortunate and connected peers were at a distinct disadvantage. While recent data demonstrate that access to computers and the Internet are clearly increasing for all demographic groups and, as previously noted, disadvantaged children are benefiting from their access at schools, a closer examination of the census data used for A Nation Online reveals worrying home disparities—disparities teachers witness everyday. Almost half of Americans still do not have Internet access at home. Only 25 percent of America's poorest households are online, compared with approximately 80 percent of homes earning over $75,000. Only 33 percent of children living in house-holds in the lowest income category use computers at home compared to 95 percent of youth in the highest income category.

Even more troubling is the fact that the gap between these groups has expanded in recent years. Similar disparities can be found among student populations:

Hispanics (32 percent) and African Americans (40 percent) lag behind Whites (60 percent) in Internet access at home, suggesting serious ethnic and racial divides. In the 21st century, sending some students to homes without a computing device—whether it be a computer, handheld device, or the like—and an Internet connection would be like, in the 20th century, sending some students home, depending on their household income or the educational level of their parents, without their textbooks—and then expecting them to do as well in the classroom.

The publication 2020 Visions: Transforming Education and Training Through Advanced Technologies, released in September 2002 by U.S. Secretary of Commerce Evans and Secretary of Education Paige, high-lights what an exciting future might expect with new innovations in instructional technology looming on the horizon. The golden age of digital learning may be around the corner if do not short-circuit the process now. Based on recent and past work in this arena, declare these 10 critical next steps must be taken if are truly to meet the sustainability challenge and take educational technology to the next level:

Professional Development

In US, the No Child Left Behind Act mandates that states and local communities spend a set percentage of their funding on teacher professional development. If done correctly, this added focus on professional development can help us accelerate the training of teachers and improve their ability to use powerful new technologies.

Professionalize technical support: One of the most neglected areas in school technology has been the support given to teachers, network administration and system design. Many large school districts have, like industry created and filled the position of Chief Information Officer. Smaller districts have outsourced their work in this area. Others have relied on already burdened teachers or students. Technical support should be given the professional status it deserves.

In an era in which results are paramount, policymakers at the state and local level must be careful not to pull the plug on their edtech investments because they see little short-term gain in student test scores. Assessments must be tied to the specific goals for which technology is used, such as reading improvement or technology literacy, and treated as an important, but not the sole, variable in the learning equation.

To truly transform education and training through advanced and emerging technologies we believe that the federal government must serve as a significant catalyst for digital content creation. Private industry cannot go it alone. One of the most promising proposals to achieve this goal is the call for the creation of a Digital Opportunity Investment Trust (DO IT). With the E-Rate covering telecommunication and networking equipment discounts and the NCLB technology block grant covering computer upgrades, software purchases and teacher training, DO IT would provide the missing link in federal investment.

Ensure all Americans have 21st Century Skills NCLB states that one goal of the federal investment in the edtech arena is to assist every student in crossing the digital divide by ensuring that every student is technologically literate by the time the student finishes the eighth grade, regardless of the student's race, ethnicity, gender, family income, geographic location, or disability. The U.S. Department of Education is investigating what this means and is taking an expansive view of the term literacy. An important component of leaving no child behind in the digital age is ensuring their parents are fully engaged in their education. To accomplish this, must ensure no parents are left behind in the dark age of illiteracy and that they have ample opportunity to develop 21st Century Skills.

Technology can play a key role in ensuring all Americans, K-12 students and adults, have 21st Century Skills. Two years ago, e-Learning: Putting a World-Class Education at the Fingertips of All Children, The National Educational Technology Plan called for ensuring equal information technology access not just in schools, but in homes and communities as well. A few states and local school districts have taken up the charge, and other policy proposals have been presented to achieve this goal. As a start, must set a national goal of ensuring every child on the reduced and free lunch programme has home access to a computing device and the Internet.

The digital learning content of the future will require greater bandwidth. A new broadband divide is emerging with the potential that some Americans will be relegated to second-class, information age citizenship. Federal policymakers must focus on policies to ensure all Americans, especially those in rural and inner city areas, have access to widely available and affordable broadband connections:

To meet the sustainability challenges outlined above states and school districts will need additional resources.

Therefore, advocate an increase in the NCLB edtech block grant to $1 billion, beginning in fiscal year 2004. In this age of accountability, states and local government will be looking for guidance on effective educational technology solutions. Through the U.S. Department of Education's new What Works Clearinghouse, research efforts, and other governmental and corporate demonstrations, a concerted effort must be made to assist them. As e-Learning advocated, initiate a systematic agenda of research and evaluation on technology applications for teaching and learning; encourage state and local evaluations of technology programmes; and support the dissemination and use of research-based information.

Around 35 percent is magnified when one considers that most federal edtech investments and the E-Rate are directed at high-poverty schools. Since the federal government launched schools on the e-learning path, it is imperative to track funding at the state and district level to see how the edtech sustainability challenge is being, or not being, met. In late 2002, leaders involved in implementing technology solutions to improve teaching and learning were faced with a bleak budget picture and changing policy climate. Educational technology (edtech) expenditures that were part of budget lines came under greater scrutiny than ever—with results expected sooner rather than later. At the same time, state and local innovations and new federal policy proposals reflected exciting opportunities to ensure that no children in the U.S. would be left behind in the information age.

Many states that benefited from the economic boom of the late-1990s suffered sharp revenue declines in the recent recession. These trends were verified in one of the states where the Benton Foundation and the Center for

Children and Technology (CCT) conducted casework: Illinois. Edtech funding was slashed in the state FY 2003 budget—receiving one of the greatest hits in terms of budget line items within the Illinois State Board of Education (ISBE) budget. School districts felt the biggest pinch in 2002 with direct state edtech grants to districts reduced by over $15 million to less than half of previous levels of $28 million. The budget for online resources for school districts was also reduced by over one-third. By most accounts, projections for the Illinois FY 2004 budget look bleak as well.

State and local innovation, as well as the budget crisis many states face, will all be affected by a redefined relationship to the federal government, which has been a significant catalyst for helping bring schools into the digital age.

In US the new Enhancing Education Through Technology Program was passed as part of the No Child Left Behind Act of 2001 (NCLB), a reauthorization of the Elementary and Secondary Education Act. It contains new provisions in how federal edtech funding gets spent. One stated new goal of the legislation is to assist every student in America in crossing the digital divide and becoming fully technology literate by the eighth grade. In proposing NCLB, and support for distant education learning programs) into a new state block grant programme. All of the savings from the program cuts were to be rolled into a revamped Technology Literacy Challenge Fund, the existing state block grant, and delivered by formula to the districts.

In attempting to sell the proposal in 2001, the administration touted its advantages to school districts: more money, less hassle in applying and more discretion in using the funds. Critics decried a lack of 'federal leadership'—in terms of a dedicated pool of funds for programs addressing national priorities, like community technology center development—and in the case of the E-Rate, the near certain loss of a substantial proportion of its support if congressional appropriations were required. In the end, the U.S. Senate pushed back, protected the E-Rate and reached a grand compromise on NCLB, which was passed in January 2002 and included the Enhancing Education Through Technology Program. This program included an edtech block grant but, because of Senate pressure, maintained Ready to Learn Television as well as the Preparing Tomorrow's Teachers to Use Technology and Community Technology Centers programs (CTC). Under NCLB, states must distribute 95 percent of their edtech block grant funds to local school districts. Fifty percent must be distributed via formula and 50 percent via competitive grants—yet another compromise forged between Congress and the administration.

Five percent of the funding allocated to state agencies in the block grant may be used for 'leadership activities' that allow them to provide districts with technical assistance, establish public-private technology acquisition initiatives to assist high-need districts, assist districts in providing professional development services, ensure special needs students gain access to technology, develop performance measurements to determine the effectiveness of edtech in helping students meet high academic standards, and collaborate with other states to develop and make available distance learning curricula. Additionally, districts must now use 25 percent of their funds for professional development in technology, with special attention given to the integration of advanced technologies into classroom curricula. One of the most pronounced NCLB changes is in the ability state and local governments will have to transfer funds between certain funding blocks. Any district that has not been identified as in need of improvement now has the ability to transfer up to 50 percent of its formula allocation under the Teacher Quality State Grants, Educational Technology State Grants, Innovative Programs or Safe and Drug-Free Schools programs to supplement its allocation under any of the programs listed above.

Thus, in states and districts where leaders feel edtech is not delivering a return on investment, half of those funds can be transferred elsewhere. Likewise, where edtech is seen as central to improvements in teaching and learning, 'new' resources are available—at the expense of other programs, of course. NCLB also requires states to test every student in grades three through eight annually in the 'basics,' i.e. reading and math. This is a significant shift from the multi-year cycle currently used. One result could be the accelerated use of information technology for assessment and data analysis that could provide information for needed changes at the classroom or school level.

6

Distance Education Outreach

The creation of a strong distance learning capability requires enormous coordinated investment in supporting infrastructure, both physical and intellectual. The physical infrastructure includes compatible 'electronic classrooms' equipped with video conferencing, television, computer, and multimedia technologies suitable for recording and perhaps transmitting the class off campus. The faculty, they claim, must become enthusiastically committed" if the distance education intervention is to be successful. When using information technologies to construct interactive learning systems, the technical components and the pedagogical components cannot be separated. Both the information technology engineers and the educators should work closely in constructing these systems. The technologist will provide the system framework and functional blocks upon which the learning courseware can be developed.

Recent developments in computer technology and software engineering have made it possible not only for delivering instructions but also for conducting laboratory experiments via the Internet. Adding experimental components on the Internet can immensely enhance instruction in distance education, especially in small states such as countries in the Caribbean, where access to facilities is limited. Formerly, instructors/teachers engaged in distance education were unable to effectively address various learning styles outside the classroom. Students were limited to paper-based courseware in which materials were primarily presented in a sequential manner according to the instructor's perception of the organization of the material. This may address the needs of some students but the needs of many others may not be satisfied because the presentation of the course material differs significantly from students preferred learning style. The use of the Internet may provide some solutions to this problem.

A series of hypertext, multimedia, and hypermedia tools would be required as the basis for the course delivery. However, one must incorporate mechanisms to ensure that students can proceed through the course materials smoothly. Instructors/teachers would therefore need to plan appropriate lesson presentations for individual students. Students would learn more efficiently because they would be able to absorb the materials rapidly, since they would be more receptive to the method of presentation.

The term distance education implies education from a distance. The basic idea is that the teachers are apart from the learners. Several generations of distance education are evident. The information technologies and the media employed, as follows:

a) Printed materials delivered by mail.

b) Analog audio and visual messages delivered by

signal transmission—broadcasting.

c) Digital data delivered by the use of microcomputers and network systems.

The first two generations of technologies employed for distance education were basically one-way communications. Teachers had to make special arrangements and efforts to receive feedback from students and no arrangements were made for students to communicate with each other during lessons. The microcomputer, in earlier stages of its development, provided opportunities for students to work more interactively with learning materials. Today, the rapid evolution of the information technology industry is enabling students to interact synchronously online and enables real-time interactions. This development challenges the academic arena to keep pace in providing students with education via modern technology.

Interacting in a Distance Education System

This review will attempt to identify a system based on certain criteria that would facilitate effective and efficient distance teaching and learning in small states. This would constitute the basis upon which electronic classrooms should be formulated. With the availability of the necessary facilities such as computers connected to the Internet, video on demand, two-way communication, and other facilities for distance education, the students should be able to do the following from any location and at their convenience:

a) Attend all classes.

b) Access all information/resources.

c) Access and use all multimedia facilities.

d) Conduct an experiment in a school laboratory.

e) Submit assignments on time, online.

f) Sit an examination.

g) Communicate with all members of the class.

h) Communicate with the teacher.

i) Make a contribution to the class and be recognized.

j) Receive timely feedback from the teacher.

k) Share ideas and information with others in the class.

l) Visit selected online libraries.

m) Print documents.

There are five major issues that must be addressed if distance education in small states is to be successfully implemented:

a) Readiness of both teachers, students and support staff (people-ware)

b) Availability of suitable equipment and facilities (hardware)

c) Availability of appropriate instructions and content (software)

d) An interesting and informative web site

e) Adequacy and reliability of the Internet Service Provider (ISP)

Peopleware

Irrespective of a technologically sophisticated system, the

absence of people or personnel who will interact intelligently with that technology will impact significantly on the usefulness of that system or technology. The distance education programme will experience success if the persons involved are interested in and motivated to learn from the system. Persons involved in such a programme will be expected to interact with computers and peripherals as well as audiovisual and other devices. In small states it is imperative that the right personnel be deployed for selected tasks in order to optimise on the benefits of using this technology and ensure some level of sustainability. A positive attitude towards the use of technology on the part of persons involved in distance education is important if this system is to be successful.

Some persons continue to think that face-to-face/ lecture is the most effective mode of instruction, although this opinion may be based on what they experienced during their academic career rather than any valid assessment procedure. Some teachers who may be willing to change or experiment with teaching strategies often find themselves locked into the 'lecture mode'. Highly motivated and competent people are required for the development and implementation of a successful distance education programme. There is need for persons involved to develop specific skills in order to effectively interact in the system or with technology. Skills such as basic keyboarding, manipulating computer software, and installing input and output peripherals on the computer are considered critical. In addition, skills for accessing and using the Internet and other computer systems in an effective way cannot be overlooked. Specialized training may be required to ensure that participants in the distance education programme are equipped to participate effectively. Instructional design skills and creativity on the part of teachers/instructors would be highly desirable, since teachers would have to understand technology and be able to integrate technology using interesting methods to motivate students. Teachers are expected to develop, select and utilize appropriate software to meet learning objectives.

Highly motivated and self-directed students are critical in distance education. It is not only desirable but also imperative that students are motivated to the extent that they will access the system on their own and do whatever is necessary to move ahead without prompting from teachers. Ther are three types of interaction in distance education—

(1) the interaction between learners and learning content;

(2) the interaction between learners and teachers;and

(3) the interaction between learners and learners—in their CORAL ((COoperative Remotely Accessible Learning)system by including the following:

   a) A course overview before each course for students.

   b) Self-test questions at the end of each instructional node.

   c) Multimedia presentations of the content.

   d) A post window for both students and teachers to leave messages.

   e) An audiovisual window to communicate with teachers and other students.

   f) An electronic whiteboard for students to exchange information online.

Persons responsible for ensuring that the system works in an efficient manner are critical. Because of the diversified nature of the technology involved it is imperative that technical personnel are equipped with a diversified background of skills that will enable them to be efficient at maintaining the system. In addition to technical skills and competencies these persons will be required to equip themselves with interpersonal and communication skills, since they may be required to communicate with users using telephone or other two-way communication devices to solve technical problems.

Hardware

Distance education cannot be implemented without inclusion of some basic hardware elements. In general, for any system, hardware can be considered to include the following elements:

— Input devices (keyboard, mouse, scanner, CD-ROM, bar code reader, joystick, touch panel, microphone)which create or input information. The origin of the information is not important. The information may be generated by the device or input from the external world directly or indirectly by the user of the system.

— Output devices that receive information then deliver it to the external world, such as monitors, printers, speakers, projection panels, and graphics plotters.

— Storage devices such as hard disk drives, removable disk drives, floppy disks, and magneto-optical disk drives that receive information and then, at a later time provide the same information upon request.

— Conversion devices such as the central processing unit (CPU)and the arithmetic logic unit (ALU)that receive information, convert it, and then provide the converted information when requested.

To implement an efficient and effective distance education system, all the hardware elements outlined must be included. It is imperative that proper hardware be used since these elements will determine the effectiveness of the intervention. Both students and teachers will need to submit and access information from remote locations, thus state-of-the-art facilities and equipment will be required. Access to appropriate equipment/hardware is a critical factor in the implementation of this type of education. It would be desirable for both teachers and students to have hardware available in their homes. This would provide greater access and hence more involvement in the learning process. However, many persons may not own equipment; consequently, public facilities would be required to provide the appropriate level of accessibility. A major problem faced by educators where hardware is concerned is cost.

High quality hardware is expensive and in many cases may be inaccessible by many students. Implementers of distant education systems, especially in small states where dollars are scarce, must be cognisant of this limitation and ensure that implementation is not plagued by unavailability of funds. An implication of high cost is that students may be denied access to equipment because of a claim that "the equipment is too expensive to allow students to destroy them. "Much value and benefits will be derived from effectively used equipment. The selection of hardware for use in distance education in small states is a critical concern. It is imperative that the right hardware be selected for the right task. Consideration should be given to criteria such as cost, obsolescence, age, impact, size, complexity, technology, materials used to manufacture, efficiency, function, durability, speed, power consumption, operational requirements, and maintenance needs.

The most expensive may not necessarily be the most appropriate. The device may be too complex for the situation or the brand name may be influencing the cost. The equipment may be old but not obsolete; conversely, it may be brand new yet obsolete. There may be a mismatch in technology as, for example, digital versus analog. The hardware may just not work because of this mismatch in technology. The materials used for manufacturing the hardware may not be appropriate. Some materials could pose health problems because of their carcinogenic nature. The operational requirements and maintenance needs may be outside the scope of the organization. Technical personnel required to maintain and repair devices may be unavailable in the state, thus causing extended delays when there is malfunction of equipment.

Software

Software is the instruction given to hardware to carry out functions. Hardware can do nothing without instructions. Irrespective of the sophistication of hardware employed, these will be useless without appropriate software. Computers require two different types of software, namely systems software and applications software. The systems software makes the computer perform basic operations such as starting up and reading disks. The applications software are programmes written to instruct the computer to perform tasks that humans want to do, such as word processing, calculations, etc.

The computer will simply not operate without software;consequently these are considered the 'fuel' for hardware. Software may either be developed and marketed commercially or developed domestically for specific purposes. In small states, the selection and use of appropriate software is of great importance. Invariably, several software packages are available with various advantages and disadvantages. In many cases, software is purchased because of one's previous knowledge of it, it is simply the one available, or the purchaser was influenced by someone who was exposed to it without critically analysing the usefulness of it. It is necessary to give careful consideration to needs before selecting software.

Knowledge of one's requirements and needs is the critical basis on which the appropriate software should be selected. A critical issue is that of cost. Most software is extremely expensive, especially special purpose software such as those needed to make distance education possible. In many instances, the cost of a software package may far exceed the hardware cost. In addition, the cost of maintenance and training needs of the software may be far in excess of the initial cost of the software.

Software programmes are constantly being upgraded and will need maintenance support. In addition to cost, the issue of availability should not be underestimated. Some developers will readily sell the first issue of a software programme to just about anyone because in most cases it is already outdated. The problem in small states is that some developers may not want to sell their most current software to foreign users. Others simply develop less adequate versions for international use and save the best for themselves.

The issue of pirating is another concern. Although many software developers have put measures in place to make pirating difficult, most software can still be easily copied and used. In many instances, persons in small states experience difficulties purchasing certain software because they are simply not available for purchase outside of the United States, Canada or other "first world " countries. This usually results in pirating, since this may be the easiest method for accessing the software.

Internet Service Provider (ISP)

The Internet is a wide area network system that links computers all over the world. This system constitutes computers in various types of organizations, including banks, libraries, museums, television stations, radio stations, departments in universities, industries, marketing companies, and numerous other organizations connected in one major network. Persons worldwide, including those in small states, can access computers from remote locations to get information, send messages, conduct meetings and conferences, purchase goods and perform many other functions. During the past decade, the Internet has placed students and teachers in a unique teaching/ learning situation. They further claimed that the major impact of the Internet on learning and instruction would be realized from the rapid growth of course materials and learning scenarios to supplement or replace text and/or handouts. Through the Internet teachers now have the potential to enhance and revolutionize the education of students at all levels. The ISP is critical to the proper functioning of distance teaching and learning, since it is through this service that most, if not all, communication and interaction will take place.

A critical issue in small states is the availability of adequate bandwidth (the channel through which information is sent)to facilitate rapid interaction within the system. It is imperative that the ISP provides a service with adequate bandwidth, since the speed of access is proportional to the number of persons accessing the Internet at any time. As the number of persons accessing the Internet increases, the efficiency of the system deteriorates, thus making access to information a very slow, tedious and boring task. It is the responsibility of the ISP to provide an economical and reliable service with adequate bandwidth to enable reasonably fast interaction with the network.

Web Site

The location on the Internet at which the distance education materials will be housed is called a web site. Web site construction in which pedagogical principles are to be addressed is a major issue. The web site creator must also address the challenges presented by rapidly changing technology. Good web sites, they claim, must contain more than a set of graphic, presentation-type images with one or two lines of text. Distance education will require high quality, content-rich, self-paced, interactive materials with clear instructions that are available on demand from any location. The material should approach a topic from several perspectives and answer the needs of students with different learning styles and at different levels of mastery. Links should be established to content areas at appropriate levels. Reading lists and problem sets should also be provided for the students to undertake off-line work. The work should be challenging and allow the students to navigate and discover for themselves.

Distance education is an emerging paradigm where learners, teachers and equipment may be at different locations. To implement successful distance education programmes in small states requires careful thought and planning. The key ingredients for success include motivated people, adequate hardware, appropriate software, an informative web site and an efficient Internet Service Provider (ISP). Using the Internet in distance education programmes opens endless possibilities in teaching-learning situations.

As we begin the 21st Century, the opportunities to apply control principles and methods are exploding. Computation, communication and sensing are becoming increasingly inexpensive and ubiquitous, with more and more devices including embedded processors, sensors, and networking hardware. This will make possible the development of machines with a degree of intelligence and reactivity that will influence nearly every aspect of life on this planet, including not just the products available, but the very environment in which we live. New developments in this increasingly information rich world will require a significant expansion of the basic tool sets of control. The complexity of the control ideas involved in the operation of the Internet, semiautonomous command and control systems, and enterprise-wide supply chain management, for example, are on the boundary of what can be done with available methods. Future applications in aerospace and transportation, information and networks, robotics and intelligent machines, biology and medicine, and materials and processing will create systems that are well beyond current levels of complexity, and new research is required to enable such developments. Control education is an integral part of the community's activities and one of its most important mechanisms for transition and impact. In 1998, the National Science Foundation (NSF) and the IEEE Control Systems Society (CSS) jointly sponsored a workshop in control engineering education which made a number of recommendations for improving control education.

New Environment for Control Education

Control is traditionally taught within the various engineering disciplines that make use of its tools, allowing a tight coupling between the methods of control and their applications in a given domain. It is also taught almost exclusively within engineering departments, especially at the undergraduate level. Graduate courses are often shared between various departments and in some places are part of the curriculum in applied mathematics or operations research (particularly in regards to optimal control and stochastic systems). This approach has served the field well for many decades and has trained an exceptional community of control practitioners and researchers. Increasingly, the modern control engineer is put in the role of being a systems engineer, responsible for linking together the many elements of a complex product or system. This requires not only a solid grounding in the framework and tools of control, but also the ability to understand the technical details of a wide variety of disciplines, including physics, chemistry, electronics, computer science, and operations research.

In addition, control is increasingly being applied outside of its traditional domains in aeronautics, chemical engineering, electrical engineering and mechanical engineering. Biologists are using ideas from control to model and analyze cells and animals; computer scientists are applying control to the design of routers and embedded software; physicists are using control to measure and modify the behavior of quantum systems, and economists are exploring the applications of feedback to markets and commerce. This change in the use of control presents a challenge to the community. In the United States, discipline boundaries within educational institutions are very strong and it is difficult to maintain a strong linkage between control educators and researchers across these boundaries.

While the control community is large and prosperous, control is typically a small part of any given discussion on curriculum since these occur within the departments. Hence it is difficult to get the resources needed to make major changes in the control curriculum. In addition, many of the new applications of control are outside of the traditional disciplines that teach control and it is hard to justify developing courses that would appeal to this broader community and integrate those new courses into the curricula of those other disciplines (e.g., biology, physics, or medicine). In order for the opportunities described elsewhere in this report to be realized, control education must be restructured to operate in this new environment. Several universities have begun to make changes in the way that control is taught and organized and these efforts provide some insights into how this restructuring might be done successfully.

Often the first step is establishing a cross-disciplinary research center, where there is a larger critical mass of control researchers. Examples include the Coordinated Science Laboratory (CSL) at the University of Illinois, Urbana-Champaign, the Center for Control Engineering and Computation (CCEC) at the University of California, Santa Barbara, and the Institute of Systems Research (ISR) at the University of Maryland. These centers coordinate research activities, organize workshops and seminars, and provide mechanisms for continuing interactions between control students and faculty in different departments.

A second step is the establishment of shared courses between the disciplines, often at the graduate level. These shared courses encourage a broader view of control since the students come from varying backgrounds. They also provide an opportunity for the larger control community at the university to establish active dialogs and provide a mechanism for sharing students and building joint research activities. Many U.S.universities have adopted this model, especially for theory oriented courses. Finally, some schools have established a separate M.S.or Ph.D.program in control. These are common in Europe, but have been much less prevalent in the United States, partly due to the traditional discipline structure around which most universities are organized. Examples in the U.S.include the Control and Dynamical Systems (CDS) program at Caltech and the Department of Systems Science and Mathematics (SSM) at Washington University.

The advantage of a separate graduate program in control is that it gives the faculty better control over the curriculum and allows a less discipline-centric approach to control. One other mechanism, popular in Europe but not yet established in the United States, is the creation of regional control alliances that build critical mass by linking together multiple universities in a geographic region. This mechanism is used very effectively, for example, in the Netherlands through the Dutch Institute of Systems and Control (DISC). With the increased availability of real-time audio, video, and digital connectivity, it is even possible to create virtual alliances -with shared classes, reading groups, and seminars on specialized topics -linking sites that are not physically near each other.

Making Control More Accessible

Coupled with this new environment for control education is the clear need to make the basic principles of feedback and control known to a wider community. As the main recommendations of the Panel illustrate, many of the future opportunities for control are in new domains and the community must develop the educational programs required to train the next generation of researchers who will address these challenges. A key element is developing new books and courses that emphasize feedback concepts and the requisite mathematics, without requiring that students come from a traditional engineering background. As more students in biology, computer science, environmental science ,physics, and other disciplines seek to learn and apply the methods of control.

The control community must explore new ways of providing the background necessary to understand the basic concepts and apply some of the advanced tools that are available. Textbooks that are aimed at this more general audience could be developed and used in courses that target first year biology or computer science graduate students, who may have very little background in continuous mathematics beyond a sophomore course in scalar ordinary diffierential equations (ODEs) and linear algebra.

The following vignette describes one attempt to make control more accessible to a broader community of research scientists and engineers. In addition to changes in specific courses on control, universities could also integrate modules on dynamics and control into their undergraduate mathematics and science curricula. Any linear algebra course could be strengthened by the addition of a short lesson on linear systems, eigenvalues, and their physical interpretation and manipulation through feedback. Freshman physics could be enriched by extending lessons on mechanical oscillators to the problem of balancing an inverted pendulum or the stability of person riding a bicycle.

The control community also must continue to implement its tools in software, so that they are accessible to users of control technology. While this has already occurred in some areas of control (such as classical and modern linear control theory), there are very few general purpose software packages available for analysis and design of nonlinear, adaptive, and hybrid systems -and many of these are not available on general purpose platforms (such as MATLAB). These tools can be used to allow non-experts to apply the most advanced techniques in the field without requiring that they first obtain a Ph.D. in control. Coupled with modeling and simulation tools, such as SIMULINK and Modelica, these packages will be particularly useful in teaching the principles of feedback by allowing exploration of relevant concepts in a variety of domains.

Broadening Control Education

In addition to changes in the curriculum designed to broaden the accessibility of control, it is important that control students also have a broader grasp of engineering, science, and mathematics. Modern control involves the development and implementation of a wide variety of very complex engineering systems and the control community has been a major source of training for people who embrace a systems perspective. The curriculum in control needs to reflect this role and provide students with the opportunity to develop the skills necessary for modern engineering and research activities. At the same time, the volume of work in control is enormous and so effort must be placed on unifying the existing knowledge base into a more compact form. There is a need for new books that systematically introduce a wide range of control techniques in an effective manner. This will be a major undertaking, but is required if future students of control are to receive a concise but thorough grounding in the fundamental principles underlying control, so that they can continue to extend the research frontier beyond its current boundary.

This occurs in part because they bring systems insight that is required for successful operation of a complex engineering product, but also because control is often the glue that ties together the components of the system (often in the form of embedded control software). Unfortunately, most control curricula do not emphasize the types of leadership and communications skills that are critical for success in these environments. A related aspect of this is strengthening the skills required for working in teams. All modern systems design is done in interdisciplinary teams and it requires certain skills to understand how to effectively interact with domain experts from a wide variety of disciplines. Courses are an effective mechanism for developing this type of insight and these should be more aggressively incorporated into control curricula at both undergraduate and graduate levels. It is also important that control students be provided with a balance between theory, applications, and computation.

In particularly, it is essential that control students build a deep domain knowledge in one or more disciplines, so that they understand how this knowledge interacts with the control methodology. Independent of the specific domain chosen, this approach provides a context for understanding other engineering domains and developing control practices and tools that bridge application areas. Shared laboratories within individual colleges or universities as well as laboratories shared among different universities could be used to implement this (with additional benefits in building cross-disciplinary and cross-university interactions). New experiments should be developed that explore the future frontiers of control, including increased use of computing, communications and networking, as well as exploration of control in novel application domains.

The Opportunities in K-12 Math and Science Education

Much as computer literacy has become commonplace in our K-12 curriculum, an understanding of the requirements, limits, and capabilities of control should become part of every scientifically literate citizen 's knowledge. Whether it is understanding why you should not pump antilock brakes or why you need to complete a regimen of antibiotics through the final pills even after symptoms disappear, an understanding of dynamics and control is essential. The development of inexpensive microprocessors, high-level computer languages, and graphical user interaces (GUIs) has made the development of test apparatus and small laboratories for rudimentary control experiments and demonstrations available within the budgets of all school districts.

The U.S. National Science Foundation recognizes the importance of its funded programs impacting the general public through its "Criterion"(Broader Impacts) in the evaluation of all submitted proposals. Because of the broad applications of control to the public good and standards of living, it is important to develop a curriculum for inclusion in pre-college (K-12) education. Currently, mathematics, science, and computer technology are taught in separate departments in the vast majority of K-12 curricula. Even sciences are compartmentalized at many schools. As at universities, the multidisciplinary nature of control is very much antithetical to that traditional thinking and structure in K-12 education. However, there is some evidence of advances toward application and integration of mathematics with science.

The Consortium for Mathematics and Its Applications (COMAP) ,which develops curriculum materials and teacher development programs in mathematics,is one example. Indeed, the leveraging of efforts with COMAP could prove fruitful and the control community could work with COMAP to enhance the current textbooks and curricula that have been developed by that consortium over the past two decades. Another resource is the Eisenhower National Clearinghouse, which maintains a database of teaching modules and resources for K-12 math and science education. In the control arena, simple experiments involving governors, thermostats, and "see-saws "can be performed as early as elementary school to illustrate the basic concepts of control. As mathematical sophistication increases through middle school and high school, quantitative analysis can be added and experimentally verified.

Some schools are beginning to teach calculus in the junior year and so a post-calculus course in applied mathematics of differential equations and dynamical systems could be created bridging chemistry, physics, biology, and mathematics. Complementary to the development of educational materials and experiments, it is also important to provide K-12 teachers with the opportunities to learn more about control. As an example of how this could be done, NASA Langley Research Center sponsored a program for teachers under the auspices of the HPCCP (High Performance Computing and Communications Program) several years ago. In this program teachers from six school districts spent 8 weeks learning the state of the art in computer hardware and software for engineering and science. Most days were spent with new material delivered in a lecture or laboratory environment in the morning with a "homework "laboratory in the afternoons. Teachers were paid a fellowship that approximated the per diem rate of entry-level teachers. This type of residential environment allowed for a total immersion in the material. In addition to becoming familiar with research-grade hardware and software and the Internet, the participants formed partnerships with each other that promoted continued collaboration throughout the coming academic years. There are numerous curriculum development and general education meetings and conferences throughout the country each year. In particular, most states have an active association of school boards and there is a National School Boards Association.

In September 1952, Scientific American published an entire issue dedicated to Automatic Control. The issue highlighted the role that control was playing in the new advancements of the time, particularly in manufacturing. The introduction of cruise control a few years later provided direct experience with the main principles of feedback. Since that time, control has become less and less visible to the general public , perhaps in part because of its success. Individuals interact with control systems and feedback many times every day, from the electronic amplifiers, tuners, and filters in television and radio, to congestion control algorithms that enable smooth Internet communications, to fiight control systems for commercial aircraft. Yet most people are unaware of control as a discipline. Other fields, such as artificial intelligence, robotics, and computer science have often been given credit for ideas whose origins lie within the control community.

There is a great need to better educate the public on the successes and opportunities for control. This public awareness is increasingly important in the face of decisions that will need to be made by government funding agencies about support for specific areas of research. The use of any number of popular outlets for communication can reach this group. Many local newspapers now have a science page or section on a weekly basis. The development of a popular level series of articles on dynamics and control could be prepared for these pages. The New York Times publishes a science section every Tuesday; a series of articles could be developed for this section spanning several weeks. A number of science museums have been developed across the nation in recent years and many of these museums are allied through professional associations.

The development of interactive dynamics and control displays for these museums would be beneficial to the museum by giving them a new exhibit and the displays reach the entire age range of the public from children through adults. Books written for non-specialized audiences in high school text-books are another mechanism for increasing the understanding of control principles in the general population. The dynamical systems community has been very successful in this regard, with many books available on chaos, complexity theory, and related concepts. Currently available books on control include books on the history of control and a book entitled 'Out of Control' that discusses many control concepts.

Multimedia Tools

There is an increasing need for educational materials that can be used in a variety of contexts for communicating the basic ideas behind control. One possible mechanism is to develop a multimedia CDROM that would include materials on the history and concepts of control, as well as tutorial material on specific topics and public domain software tools for control analysis and design. The fluid mechanics community has recently developed such a multimedia CDROM that can be used as a supplement to traditional courses in fluid mechanics. It contains historical accounts of fluid mechanics, videos and animations of important concepts in fluids, and detailed descriptions of fundamental phenomena. One of the most sophisticated tools demonstrates ro-bust stabilization, including the ability to specify an uncertainty weight by moving poles and zeros of the weighting transfer function with the mouse. A controller can then be designed by dragging the compensator poles and zeros to achieve robust, closed loop stability.

Software

One of the success stories of control is the wide availability of commercial software for modeling, analyzing, designing, and implementing control systems. The Controls Toolbox in MATLAB provides the basic tools of classical and modern control and many other toolboxes are available for more implementing more specialized theory. These toolboxes are used throughout academia, government, and industry and give students, researchers, and practitioners access to powerful tools that have been carefully designed and tested. One area where substantial progress has been made recently is in modeling tools, where there are several software packages available for modeling, simulation, and analysis of large-scale, complex systems. Additional tools are needed for control-oriented modeling, analysis, and synthesis of nonlinear and hybrid systems, particularly those that have a strong interaction with information rich systems, where good scaling properties are required. As yet, there is not a standard representational framework for such systems (beyond symbolic representations) and hence software tools for nonlinear or hybrid analysis are much less used than those for linear systems. One of the main issues here is to capture the relevant dynamics in a framework that is amenable to computation. Analysis and synthesis must be able to handle systems containing table lookups, logical elements, time delays, and models for computation and communication elements.

Interaction with industry is an important component of any engineering research or educational activity. The control community has a strong history of impact on many important problems and industry involvement will be critical for the eventual success of the future directions. This could occur through cooperative Ph.D.programs where industrial researchers are supported half by companies and half by universities to pursue Ph.D.'s (full-time), with the benefits of bringing more understanding of real-world problems to the university and transferring the latest developments back to industry. In addition, industry leaders and executives from the control community should continue to interact with the community and help communicate the needs of their constituencies. The NSF/CSS workshop also recognized the important role that industry plays and recommended that educators and funding organizations encourage the development of WWW-based initiatives for technical information dissemination to industrial users of control systems and encourage the transfer of practical industrial experience to the classroom.

The further recommended that cooperative efforts between academia and industry, especially in terms of educational matters, be significantly expanded. The International Federation of Automatic Control (IFAC) is creating a collection of IFAC Professional Briefs. These Professional Briefs are aimed at a readership of general professional control engineers (industrial and academic), rather than specialist researchers. The briefs provide an introduction and overview of a 'hot topic,' illustrative results, and a sketch of the underlying theory, with special attention given to providing information sources such as useful Internet sites, books, papers, etc.

Technology Support Implications

This matter will show that transitioning from face-to-face learning to online learning has several technological and support issues that should be carefully examined and understood, if the process is to be successful. The Campus Information Technology Services Department (CITS) of the UWI first became involved in this exercise in the second quarter of 1999. CITS was invited by the Instructional Development Unit (IDU) on the campus to partner with that department in delivering a programme on Web-based training. The objective of the programme was to introduce a specific tool used for the delivery of asynchronous learning to a small cross section of the faculty and library personnel. It is a sophisticated Web enabled course management system comprising a database that stores all information on users, content and classes, and allows access via the Internet to authenticated users.

Participants—represented by faculty and staff It is important to note that at this stage the campus had not taken a decision to officially begin using Web-based learning as an alternative to the traditional approach for the delivery of courses. Therefore there was no specific budget allocation for this exercise. This is a typical issue of funding and financial support for these types of programme in small states.

The approach by the IDU was therefore to introduce the campus community to a pedagogy that was based upon collaborative learning approaches that recognize the power of Internet technology as a viable alternative. To this end, faculty and library staff were initially polled to ascertain their interest in pursuing such a programme. The response was very favourable; as a matter of fact, it appeared that if such a programme were delivered on the campus it would be oversubscribed and therefore would have to be carefully managed. Next the IDU, as the primary driver of the process, sought and acquired the required funding to conduct the programme. Funds were required for the following:

— Fees for the trainer

— Airfare and accommodation for the trainer

— Acquiring the software

— Administrative training charges

The Role and Involvement of the CITS CITS, as the name suggests, has been given the mandate to manage the Campus's IT. This involves supporting the missions of the Campus and the University through planning, implementing, operating and maintaining systems to enhance the Campus's effectiveness. " As a result, the department was approached to partner with the IDU to provide technical assistance and support for the hardware and software needed to facilitate the programme. As one would imagine, technical issues associated with the delivery of distance education are of paramount importance in restructuring traditional teaching and learning. While technology on its own cannot drive the change process needed in education system today, a good understanding of both the opportunities and the problems/challenges created by attempting to integrate the technology with the pedagogy is needed to effect the desired outcomes. Currently one of the serious problems and the primary impediment to the integration of technology into higher education instruction is the lack of an efficient faculty support system for instructional technology.

In small states, it is even more of a challenge due to the inadequacy of support both locally and globally. This is so primarily because support personnel are not product specialists as their counterparts are in developed or larger countries. Over the last five years or so, application support has become very decentralized, with operational departments opting to provide hardware, software and infrastructure support to end users of the application systems used to support the department's core functions. With respect to hardware support, here too there is a mix of support strategies. The campus technology infrastructure is supported by CITS, while the faculties and departments generally support their own local area networks (LANs), and end user hardware. Support for the application hardware (servers) is generally provided by the faculties and department; however, this situation is being revisited, with some departments opting to have CITS provide their server support.

The Role and Involvement of the Participants

Only full-time members of faculty and library staff were eligible to participate in the programme.

They were selected based on the following criteria:

— *Interest expressed:* A commitment to attending the entire programme if selected (Since space was limited) early registration Participants were expected to have a working knowledge of the operating system (which was Windows NT on this campus) and a productivity tool such as MS Word or MS PowerPoint. " It is difficult to conceive of pedagogically sound ways to apply technology when you are not familiar with it". Apart from those two basic requirements, participants were not required to have any other technical skills. They were also asked to prepare some type of course information, including a draft outline and some content, which would be used throughout the training.

Installing the software and configuring the lab for the training was a fairly straightforward process. This was handled in advance of the training using pre-training implementation instructions sent by the trainer. Although it was envisaged that the trainer would provide the system administration functions for the training, the need, however, for these skills to be transferred to a local support person was quickly recognized. This was, yet again, an area in which the support issues began to challenge CITS. Two individuals were identified from CITS to be trained on the system. However, neither could be dedicated to support persons, nor troubleshoot and resolve issues as they arose either during or after the training. One individual was assigned to work with the

IDU and the participants, manage and coordinate the technical aspects of the training, get an understanding of the product, and determine how this or similar products could be used on the campus. The other individual was assigned the work of configuring the lab and installing the application and other software needed for the training.

Administering the system involves the following:

— Creating TopClass users, including instructors, students, and other administrators

— Assigning privileges to the instructors

— Organizing students and instructors into classes

— Making course material available to students

— Maintaining the TopClass system

The first challenge came with respect to compatibility between the lab's hardware environment and the version of the software installed. As with most technical issues, a fair amount of time has to be spent testing and troubleshooting the system to ensure configuration and functionality. Although the lab's hardware configuration matched the requirements specified by the software vendors, there were a number of interruptions during the training to try to resolve configuration problems. These interruptions caused general disruptiveness, loss of concentration by participants, and resulted in the inability of some participants to complete their assignments. Since Web-based training was neither a core function nor a mission critical application for the campus, no additional resources were sought or deployed to work on these problems.

The training was successful in achieving its objective: the interest of the participants was ignited. The new challenge was how to sustain this interest. The participants agreed that they must continue to use and become familiar with the product if any true benefits were to be realized. It was therefore agreed that the training lab would remain available to the participants at specified times to encourage this activity.

Ongoing Access and Post Training Support

Although the training lab remained operational, it soon became quite clear to the participants that there were problems of access to use the system and the provision of support for problems encountered with the software. Access to the system was permitted only from the lab venue and was very restrictive and inconvenient. Participants would have preferred to access the system from their personal computers in their offices or homes. The configuration and installation of the application for individual participants was soon abandoned. Although performing these functions was assigned to a single technical support person, priority had to be given to "real" CITS work, and left no time for these activities that were considered extraneous. Moreover, having successfully installed the application on the participant's machine, another problem arose: that of access to the data on the server via the Internet. This was further complicated by the fact that the server, in its initial configuration, was not set up to be accessed from outside the lab environment.

The server had to be redeployed so that the data could be used and the Internet could be accessed. This took time and resources and resulted in some delays. Furthermore, redeploying the server identified the need for purchasing additional, though inexpensive, software. By the time the server was reinstalled to an area in CITS where it could be accessed via the Internet, only two of the original forty participants remained committed to continue. Eventually, only one of these two participants decided to move forward with a pilot/test case, in spite of the support concerns. Support problems soon rose to a new dimension.

The last twelve months provided a framework for beginning to understand the technology and support implications for small states in delivering online courses. As a result, some of these are already being addressed for the new academic year. New support personnel are currently being recruited and will be trained to facilitate ongoing support. Although it is recognized that support will eventually be required 24 by 7, the present demand is not sufficient to justify the introduction of extended hours initially. It is envisaged, however, a help desk facility; e-mail help-line; establishment of an in-house user group or association with external user groups; and on-going training for faculty and student users.

Bibliography

Burns, Richard W. & Gary D. Brooks, (eds.), 1970. *Curriculum Design in a Changing Society*. Educational Technology Publications, Englewood Cliffs, NJ.

Butler, H.J. 'Library Instruction in an Electronic Classroom" In Linda Shirato (ed.), *What Is Good Instruction Now? Library Instruction for the 90s*. Ann Arbor, MI: Pierian Press, 1993.

Clabaugh, S. (ed.), Allen, R.L., Ault, D.K., Bowen, J.T., DeWitt, B.B., Francis, J., Kerstetter, J.P., & Sodergren, R.T. *Design of General Purpose Classrooms, Lecture Halls, and Seminar Rooms*, College Park, MD: Educational Technology Center, University of Maryland, 1993.

Conway, K., Epstein, S.L., Griffin, S., Luttell, D.R., & Wilson, J., 1994. *Classroom Design With Technology in Mind* Satellite Broadcast, Videocassette Recording. Raleigh, NC: Institute for Academic Technology.

Dwyer, D. C., Ringstaff, C. and Sandholt, J. H. 1991 "Changes in Teachers' Beliefs and Practices in Technology-Rich Classrooms." Educational Leadership, 48, 45-52.

Dyrli, O. E. and Kinnaman, D. E. 1993 "Developing a Technology- Powered Curriculum." *Technology and Learning*, 15, 46-51.

Farber, E.I. BI and Library Instruction: Some Observations. *Reference Librarian*, (10), 5-13, 1984.

Knirk, F.G. *Instructional Facilities for the Information Age*. Syracuse, NY: ERIC Clearinghouse on Information Resources, 1987.

Lieberman, D. A. & Linn, M. C. 1991. "Learning to learn revisited: Computers and the development of self-directed learning skills". *Journal of Research on Computing in Education*, 373-395.

Pearlman, R. 1991. "Restructuring with Technology: A Tour of Schools Where It's Happening." *Technology and Learning*, 11, 30-34.

Pearlman, R. 1993. "Designing the New American Schools." *Communications of the ACM*, 36, 46-49.

Schreiner, R. "Electronic classrooms", *Bibliographic Instruction Discussion Group*, 24 January 1994.

Solaway, E. (1993) "Technology in Education: Introduction." *Communications of the ACM*, 36, 30-31.

Strommern, E, F. and Lincoln, B. 1992. "Constructivism, Technology and the Future of Classroom Learning." *Education and Urban Society*, 24, 466-473.

Swan, K. and Mitrani, M. 1993. "The Changing Nature of Teaching and Learning in Computer-Based Classrooms." *Journal of Research on Computing in Education*, 26, 40-54.

Van Dusen, L. M., and Worthen, B. R. (1995) "Can Integrated Instructional Technology Transform the Classroom?" *Educational Leadership*, 53, 28-33.

Van Horn, R. (1991) *Advanced Technology in Education*, Brooks/ Cole Publishing Company.

Williams, W.., "Designing a lab/classroom", *Educational Technology*, 8 January 1994.

Wilson, D. L., "Universities Wrestle With the Design of Tomorrow's High-Tech Classroom", *The Chronicle of Higher Education*, 39(28), A19-A20., 1993.

Wilson, D.L. 1993. Universities Wrestle With the Design of Tomorrow's High-Tech Classroom. *The Chronicle of Higher Education*, 39(28), A19-A20.

Wright, C, &, Friend, L. 1992. Ergonomics for Online Searching. *Online*, *16*(3), 13-15, 17-20, 22-27.

Index